Relatives Raising Children

# Relatives
# Raising
# Children
## An Overview of Kinship Care

DISCARD

*Edited by Joseph Crumbley & Robert L. Little*
*CWLA Press • Washington, DC*

*CWLA Press is an imprint of the Child Welfare League of America.*

CHILD WELFARE LEAGUE OF AMERICA, INC.
440 First Street, NW, Third Floor, Washington, DC 20001-2085
e-mail: books@cwla.org

CURRENT PRINTING (last digit)
10 9 8 7 6 5 4 3

Cover design by Jennifer R. Geanakos
Text design by Eve Malakoff-Klein

Printed in the United States of America

ISBN # 0–87868–684–3

*Library of Congress Cataloging-in-Publication Data*
Relatives raising children : an overview of kinship care / edited by
    Joseph Crumbley & Robert L. Little.
            p.      cm.
        Includes bibliographical references (p.    )
        ISBN 0–87868–684–3 (pbk.)
            1. Kinship care--United States.    2. Foster parents--United States.
        3. Foster children--United States.        4. Family social work--United
        States.            I. Crumbley, Joseph.    II. Little, Robert L., 1938–
        HV881.R53    1997
        362.73'3'0973--dc21                                                97–25669

# Contents

# About the Authors

*Joseph Crumbley,* D.S.W., is a Family Therapist in private practice as a consultant and family therapist. His areas of specialization include pre- and postadoptive therapy, chemical dependency, couples therapy, and physical and sexual abuse therapy. In the area of kinship care, he has been a consultant to the Los Angeles County Kinship Care Program, the Child Welfare Institute, the Child Welfare League of America, the Spaulding Center, and the Philadelphia Society for Services to Children Kinship Care Program.

Dr. Crumbley received his master's degree and doctorate from the University of Pennsylvania. In addition to his role as co-editor of this volume, he is the author of Chapters One through Five and of the Kinship Care Case Study.

*Robert L. Little,* M.S.W., ACSW, is president and CEO of R. Langdon Co., a human services consulting firm specializing in community and minority social service issues. Until January 1994, he served as the Executive Deputy Commissioner of the City of New York's Human Resources Administration and as Commissioner of New York City's Child Welfare Administration. With over 30 years of experience in various state and local government agencies and social service organizations, he has a broad range of expertise in inter- and intragovernmental relations, public sector policy, and crisis management.

Mr. Little received his undergraduate and graduate degrees from Michigan State University's School of Social Work. In addition to his role as co-editor of this volume, Mr. Little is the author of Chapter Seven.

*Frank Cervone,* J.D., is Executive Director of the Support Center for Child Advocates, a pro bono program that represents abused and neglected children in Philadelphia. He serves as co-chair of the American Bar Association Section on Litigation Task Force on Children. Prior to his work at the Support Center, he was a Staff Attorney at Delaware County Legal Assistance Association and Adjunct Clinical Professor in domestic abuse and child support litigation at Villanova University School of Law. Mr. Cervone is a graduate of the University of Pennsylvania and Villanova University School of Law and is the co-author of Chapter Six.

*Rebecca R. Thomas,* J.D., is a Staff Attorney with the Support Center for Child Advocates and is responsible for "Kid's 'n Kin: The Caregiving Program," a joint venture with the Philadelphia Society for Services to Children that provides in-home legal and social services to relative caregivers and their kinship children. Ms. Thomas is a graduate of Dartmouth College and Stanford University School of Law, and is the co-author of Chapter Six.

# *Foreword*

Although people, when asked, will consistently identify "family" as more important than anything else, their understanding of the meaning of family will differ. For some, *family* means parents and children. For others, *family* includes a large extended network of relatives and for others still, *family* extends beyond blood ties to feelings of kinship with significant people such as godparents, tribe or clan members, and best friends. Some of these differences in perspective relate to cultural influences, others come from more recent traditions—customs defined by each family.

However it is defined, the concept of family brings with it a sense of belonging, caring, and duty toward family members—a sense that propels individuals to step forward and take responsibility for raising a child when the child's parents are unable to do so.

Kinship care—the full-time parenting of children by kin—is a phenomenon that has been practiced informally throughout history in certain cultures and is well known to family service and child welfare agencies. In *Kinship Care: A Natural Bridge* [1994], the Child Welfare League of America highlights the potential that kinship care holds for children in need of placement, noting that it

- enables children to live with persons whom they know and trust;

- reduces the trauma children may experience when they are placed with persons who are initially unknown to them;

- reinforces children's sense of identity and self-esteem, which flows from knowing their family history and culture;

- facilitates children's connections to their siblings; and

-  strengthens the ability of families to give children the support they need.

The use of kinship care as a formal child welfare service has expanded markedly in recent years, reflecting the increasing number of parents who are unable to care for their children due to substance abuse, HIV/AIDS, physical and mental illness, homelessness, or poverty. Increasingly, agencies serving families are becoming involved in the decision to place children with kin, the monitoring of kinship family arrangements for child protection and safety, and the provision of counseling and case management services to all segments of the kinship family; and in the planning necessary to achieve legal permanence for the children.

*Relatives Raising Children: An Overview of Kinship Care* provides an in-depth understanding of the benefits and challenges of kinship care, assessment and intervention strategies, legal and policy issues, and other considerations. Our hope is that it will help family service practitioners, helping agencies, policymakers, and caring people of diverse callings to move toward a better understanding of, and development of more effective and supporting services to kinship families.

DANA BURDNELL WILSON
*Director, Cultural Competence*
*& Kinship Care Services*
*Child Welfare League of America*

# *Introduction*

Kinship care is not a new concept. Relatives (and extended family and friends)* have been caring for children in the absence of parents for centuries, functioning as a secondary support to the immediate or nuclear family (i.e., mother and/or father). The Child Welfare League of America defines kinship care as:

> the full-time nurturing and protection of children who must be separated from their parents by relatives, members of their tribe or clans, godparents, stepparents, or other adults who have a kinship bond with a child. [CWLA 1994: 2]

What is new is the increase in the number of relatives and kinship families becoming permanent or long-term primary caregivers. This increase in the amount of time children spend in kinship care has been attributed to parallel increases in divorce, marital separation, alcohol and other drug abuse, parental incarceration, child abuse, and AIDS-related parental incapacity or mortality [Wilson & Chipungu 1996]. Consequently, courts, communities, families, and child welfare systems are beginning to recognize and formalize the legal status of relatives and kinship families as primary caregivers. According to the U.S. Bureau of the Census [1993], approximately 4.3 million children lived with relatives

---

* The terms *relative caregiver* and *kinship caregiver* are used interchangeably throughout this book. The term *parent* is used in reference to the child's biological parent, or the parent from whom the child was separated and placed in kinship care.

other than or in addition to their parents. While most of these children lived with their mothers in the homes of relatives, some 878,000 lived apart from both of their parents in their grandparents' homes. An unknown number lived apart from both of their parents with relatives other than grandparents.

The rapid growth of kinship care has caught many child welfare agencies off guard [CWLA 1994]. Consequently, a substantive knowledge base for policy, program, and practice guidelines to assist agencies in developing and implementing quality kinship care programs is lacking. Professionals, agencies, institutions, and organizations need answers to questions such as:

- What are the social, legal, financial, and emotional needs of kinship families?

- What services and supports do kinship families need?

- What policies and practices are necessary to ensure adequate responses to the needs of kinship families?

- What are the assets of, limits on, and challenges to kinship care providers and kinship families?

- What roles should biological parents play in relation to kinship families?

- What is the emotional impact of kinship care on the child, biological parent, and kinship caregiver's relationships?

- What are the legal rights of kinship care providers?

- How can professionals help families access financial, social, and legal systems?

- How can professionals assess and prepare individuals to qualify as and become kinship care providers?

- What are the typical questions kinship caregivers have about kinship care?

*Relatives Raising Children* provides professionals, agencies, institutions, communities, and organizations with the information they need to develop and provide services to kinship caregivers, kinship families, children, and biological parents.

- Chapter One, "The Benefits and Challenges of Kinship Care," compares relative or kinship care to traditional family foster care, and outlines the characteristics of kinship care that necessitate changes in outlook and practice.

- Chapter Two, "Clinical Concepts," analyzes the clinical issues that must be considered in serving children, parents, and kinship caregivers. These issues—losses specific to kinship families, confusion about redefining roles and boundaries, split/dual loyalties, guilt and anger, and embarrassment—all have implications for the effective provisions of services to kinship families.

- Chapters Three and Four provide guidance on practice with kinship families. Chapter Three, "Assessment and Intervention," advocates a comprehensive approach, and discusses the intrafamilial relationships that must be considered in addition to the relationships with the service worker. Chapter Four, "Case Management," addresses the managing of clinical services to the family, as well as financial, legal, health, and educational services.

- The kinship care tradition spans cultural, racial, socioeconomic, and geographic boundaries. Chapter Five, "Race, Culture, and Other Special Considerations," considers the effect of culturally based child-rearing practices, gender roles, and hierarchy of authority on practice with kinship families, as well as the impact of parental incarceration, substance abuse, and HIV/AIDS.

- Chapter Six, "Legal Relationships," looks at the legal rights, responsibilities, and status of kinship families, caregivers, parents, and children. The child's status in relation to the kinship caregiver can make a significant difference in the availability of supportive funding and services, and in lines of responsibility and authority.

- Chapter Seven, "Federal and State Policy and Program Issues," discusses federal and state issues for program and policy development and examines the philosophy and values underlying the provision of financial support to kinship families, the emerging federal role, state policy directions, and permanency planning. The chapter also identifies the programs, structures, components, and staffing essential to providing services to kinship families and concludes with a list of action steps for state and local planners.

The Appendix, "A Kinship Care Case Study," applies the materials presented throughout *Relatives Raising Children* to an example drawn from actual practice.

# Chapter One
# *The Benefits and Challenges of Kinship Care*

The placement of a child with relatives or kin when out-of-home care is necessary brings with it both benefits and challenges, and requires professionals to adjust their approach to practice with these children.

## The Benefits of Kinship Care

Family preservation is the most obvious benefit of kinship care. Kinship care preserves the continuity of care, relationship, and environment that are essential to a child's overall well-being. Kinship care also maintains the family system as the primary provider of care for the child, and forestalls the child becoming an institutional and social responsibility.

A child's psychological and emotional stability are more easily maintained when he or she remains in the family system. Children in kinship care are better able to avoid the multiple emotional problems associated with nonrelative placements (i.e., family foster care and adoption) such as separation anxiety, adjustment reactions, attachment disorders, or conduct disorders.

Kinship caregivers can intercept and help the child avoid family life cycle interruptions and family legacies such as substance abuse, child maltreatment, incarceration, and codependency. More importantly, kinship family members can establish new traditions, goals, and value systems for themselves and the children in their care. Children are usually more receptive to learning new behaviors from familiar family and friends than from nonrelated role models. Their attachment to and identification with the family and its role models expedites the learning process.

Children placed in kinship care are often better able to address unresolved family issues and traumas. This enhanced ability to confront the source of problems or traumas can minimize the steps of recollection, identification, disclosure, and confrontation associated with the healing process. Families become part of the children's natural healing systems. In healing its members, the family heals itself, and is more likely to produce healthier individuals, complete family life cycles, and build positive legacies.

Being removed from theit parents predisposes children to feelings of abandonment and rejection. These feelings are minimized for children who are placed with family members or kin. Kinship placements facilitate the development of positive self-image, self-esteem, and identity, and consequently, may help children avoid the double jeopardy of feeling abandoned by both parents and family. Children placed in kinship care continue to feel a sense of belonging, worth, history, and value to others.

## The Challenges of Kinship Care

In kinship care, role and boundary confusion can be problematic for the child, caregiver, and parent. Assuming new roles and relinquishing old ones can be as challenging for adults as it is for children.

Adults may be threatened by the need to reestablishing a hierarchy for decision making, authority, and parenting. Children may find it a challenge to accept new hierarchies and roles as well. "Who's the boss?" is a common question in kinship families. The presence of transient family members and multiple households contributes to the confusion.

Kinship families are also challenged by the need to minimize the impact of family legacies and life cycles on the child. Children carry with them their family history, traditions, and legacies, even when they are placed outside of their families. Kinship placements tend to reinforce legacies and life cycles because of family loyalties, attachments, object identification, and the presence of family role models. Children and family members may find it especially challenging to interrupt legacies and life cycles when the child remains in the family system.

Alternative permanency planning is a common concern in kinship families. Most kinship caregivers are grandmothers [CWLA 1994]. Associated with their age are issues of morbidity and mortality—issues that are not commonly a concern with nonrelative caregivers. Kinship caregivers may need to develop alternative permanency plans in anticipation of their absence or death. Surrogate support systems and respite plans may also need to be developed to provide relief to the relative when needed due to physical or emotional limitations, stress, or health care needs (i.e., medical appointments, stress management, physically challenging activities with the child).

## Characteristics of Kinship Placements

The characteristics that differentiate kinship care from nonrelative care will change the way the child, family, and caregiver interact, and the practitioner's approach to them. These characteristics include: (1) the parent's history with the caregiving family (adoptive, foster, or kinship); (2) the parent's future involvement with the caregiving family; (3) the impact of past legacies on the caregiving family; (4) the configuration of the caregiving family in which the child lives; (5) alternative permanency planning by the families; and (6) clinical issues.

### Shared History

The presence and quality of a shared history between the parent and the kinship caregiver can either positively or negatively influenced their relationship. In nonrelative placements, the parent and caregiver typically have not had a history with each other prior to the child's placement, nor has the parent usually been involved with the nonrelative caregiver's family. In kinship placements, however, the child's parent and the caregiver may have a history of contacts that predate the child's birth. The parent may also have had a relationship with the kinship caregiver's family. The caregiver's attitudes and feeling toward the parent may be influenced by the caregiver family's history and involvement with the parent.

In kinship placements, the parent's *family* may also share a past with the caregiver's *family* (i.e., maternal and paternal grandparents, siblings, aunts, or uncles). This history and past contact among immediate and extended families rarely occurs in nonrelative placements. The parent/caregiver relationship is more subject in relative placements to family influences and loyalties than in nonrelative placements.

In kinship adoptions, the parent has usually had extensive contact with the child, contact that may or may not have been present in nonrelative adoptive placements, depending on the age of the child and type of placement. The age of the child and type of placement usually also determines the intensity and clarity of the child's memory.

### Future Interactions

The parent and kinship caregiver are more likely to be involved with each other in the future in kinship placements as compared to nonrelative placements. This may be due to judicial stipulations or to the existence of family relationships (positive or negative) apart from those involving the child.

Future involvement is also likely between the parent and the kinship caregiver's immediate or extended family. The literature suggests that grandparents are usually the caregivers in kinship placements. Therefore, the child's parents will likely continue to have interactions (positive or negative) with the grandparents (the parents' parents), siblings, aunts, and uncles. The likelihood of these future interactions is reinforced by the family's shared history.

The immediate families of the parent and the kinship caregiver (i.e., maternal and paternal grandparents, aunts, uncles, cousins) are more likely to have future contact or involvement in kinship placement than in nonrelative placements. Their relationship to the child naturally elicits continued involvement, even in the face of court-ordered termination of parental rights or restraining orders forbidding contact. Again, this ongoing involvement is frequently due to the existence of family relationships that predate the child's placement or birth.

In relative placements, the child's involvement with and memories of the parent are more likely to be reinforced than in nonrelative placement. In spite of court orders, kinship caregivers frequently refer to or remind children of their parents, either positively and/or negatively). The references may be as simple as: "You look like your dad, " "I saw your mom yesterday," "Here's a birthday card from your parents," or "Your mom said you better listen to grandmom."

The parent's and caregiver's redefinition and exchange or roles are likely to be more complicated in kinship placements than in nonrelative placements. Nonrelative caregivers begin in a parental role. In kinship care, however, caregivers frequently need to assume parental roles that may not have existed with the child prior to placement. Once established, the caregiver's and parent's roles may not need redefining in nonrelative placements. In kinship placements, however, preexisting roles, relationships, and hierarchies do require redefining. In fact, resistance to changing preexisting relationships and roles may be more of a challenge in relative than in nonrelative placements.

## Legacies

*Legacies* are patterns of behavior, values, and traditions that are passed on between generations and among family members. Children's legacies are more easily reinforced in relative placements than in nonrelative placements. Although the family's legacies can certainly be reinforced in nonrelative placements if they coincide with those of the caregiving family, the presence of predecessors, role models, attachments, and loyalty predispose children to repeat legacies in kinship care. In addition, legacies are more likely to be present in the home of relatives than in those of nonrelatives.

Interrupting the child's exposure to legacies can be difficult in kinship placements. Even though the relative caregiver may interrupt the cycle, other family and household members may repeat the legacies. The child's continued exposure to family legacies is of particular concern in multigenerational and multifamily households.

## Family and Household Configuration

Children in kinship placements are more likely to reside in multigenerational families than children in nonrelative placements. Statistics [Wilson & Chipungu 1996] indicate that grandparents are usually the caregivers in kinship placements and that the child is usually at least two generations removed from the relative. The relative's age may result in other family members living in the home and providing assistance and support.

The child in kinship care is more likely to be subject to multiple primary and secondary caregivers than the child in a nonrelative placement, as the configuration of multigenerational and multifamily households is conducive to multiple caregivers. These configurations and patterns of child care may also be a result of family traditions, cultures, and necessity, such as the cost of day care.

## Alternative Permanency Planning

Morbidity and mortality are more immediate concerns for caregivers providing kinship placement than for those providing nonrelative placement. Kinship caregivers tend to be older than nonrelative caregivers. Elderly kinship caregivers will likely encounter issues of morbidity and mortality sooner than younger family foster caregivers. Therefore, alternative permanency plans need to be developed sooner for kinship caregivers than for nonrelative caregivers. Family members may also need to become involved sooner with alternative planning in kinship versus nonrelative placements.

Respite planning may need to be addressed much sooner and more extensively in kinship placements than in nonrelative placements, as an elderly caregiver's age may lower his or her physical and emotional thresholds. When a child is placed in kinship care, additional caregivers may need to be identified to provide short-term relief.

## Clinical Issues

In kinship placements, the child's problems are viewed as symptomatic of and originating from the family. Nonrelative families are not considered the source of the child's problem when the child is initially placed, due to the lack of a previous history with the child.

Intervention strategies in nonrelative placements initially focus on the child and the role of the caregiving family as part of the intervention. In kinship placements, the focus of intervention may be the child and the family (i.e., legacies). The goal is to empower family members so that they can help the child. Empowerment and intervention strategies may include the coordination of individual and family therapeutic, financial, legal, housing, medical, and educational services.

Although many of the same clinical issues apply to relative and nonrelative placements, they may make themselves apparent in different ways. For example, kinship caregivers and adoptive parents both have fantasies. However, the kinship caregiver's fantasy may be the reunification of the child with his or her mother. An adoptive parent's initial fantasy will be just the opposite. Though the concepts are the same, the application and interpretation of behaviors are different. A more detailed application of clinical concepts in kinship families can be found in Chapter Two.

# Chapter Two
# Clinical Concepts

This chapter's discussion of clinical issues impacting the relative caregivers, child, and biological parents is based on several theoretical models and frameworks, including systems theory, attachment theory, and various models of human growth and development. Conceptual references are drawn from intergenerational models, life cycles, family therapy, and models of codependency.

## Clinical Issues for the Kinship Caregiver

### Loss

Relatives who take on the care of their kinship children may experience multiple losses. These losses may take many forms: interrupted life cycles (i.e., postponed plans for retirement or second careers, delayed goals), intrusions on space and privacy, and changes in the caregiver's roles and relationships with the children and the children's parents. Although the majority of relative caregivers are grandparents, aunts, uncles, cousins, and siblings providing kinship care can also experience these losses.

The elderly caregivers who comprise the majority of kinship caregivers are usually in the later stages of the life cycle. They may be couples with a lifelong commitment to each other, or widowed or single. They may be planning for retirement, or looking forward to a second career or relocation. Whether the postponement of their plans and life stages is temporary or permanent will depend on the age of the children for whom they will care, their own age, and the permanency of the children's residency. Elderly caregivers who state that, "We'll be raising children for the rest of our lives" may not be speaking figuratively.

Relatives who take on the care of children frequently suffer a loss of space and privacy. Depending on the age of the children, kinship caregivers may need to initiate a second nesting process in preparation for the return of children to their homes, "child-proofing" their homes and putting away fragile and delicate possessions such as treasured books, antiques, and crystal.

The priorities of relative caregivers must also shift as the needs of the children take precedence over those of the caregiver. With the change in priorities comes a change in and loss of relationships as well.

Many relative caregivers may now enjoy having the kind of relationships with nieces, nephews, and grandchildren that they may not have had with their own children due to their roles as parents. Grandparents frequently joke about being able to enjoy the children and then "send them home." Relatives who take on the role of parent, however, must also take on the role of "the heavy" and become disciplinarians.

Kinship caregivers also experience the loss of their peer relationship with the child's parent. As primary caregiver, the relative now has more authority over the child than the parent. Consequently, the caregiver and parent are no longer peers in relation to the child, or to each other.

Too often, caregivers deny, minimize and repress their losses out of feelings of obligation, loyalty, and responsibility to the child or parent. Unfortunately, professionals may overlook or not adequately assess caregiver loss as they strive to achieve some semblance of family preservation. The ability to acknowledge and inventory losses, however, is necessary in order to determine the caregiver's (1) pain, hurt, and stresses; (2) thresholds and capabilities; and (3) limits and tolerance for future losses, stresses, pressures, and responsibilities. To avoid this inventory and assessment of losses places children at risk of further family disruption and relatives at risk of becoming emotionally, financially, and physically overextended.

## *Redefining Roles and Boundaries*

Changes in the caregiver's roles and boundaries occur not only with respect to the child, but also with respect to the child's parent. Relationships with the parent are redefined as the kinship caregiver undergoes a transformation from supporter to primary caregiver, from advisor to decision maker, and from friend or peer to authority figure.

The relative caregiver may be perceived by the parent as a competitor for his or her authority and relationship with the child. The caregiver's and parent's relationship can become hierarchical and adversarial, especially if the caregiver's legal authority extends not only to the child, but also to the biological parent. For example, the relative may have the authority to determine if, when, how, and where the parent may visit or have contact with the child.

Children may have difficulty adjusting to these changes in roles and boundaries. Now that the grandparent is in a parental role, the child's prior role as "grandpop's little helper" may need to change, as will the child's perception of the grandparent or elderly caregiver as fragile and dependent. Boundaries will shift and the child may feel confused and resentful toward relatives "bossing" him or her around and telling the parents what they can or can not do.

## *Guilt and Embarrassment*

Kinship caregivers may experience guilt and embarrassment if they feel responsible for the parent's loss of the child. Many relatives (especially grandparents) wonder if the parents' problems are a result of their own failure as relatives (or as parents).

A second source of guilt and embarrassment for kinship caregivers is the feeling that they are contributing to the family disruption by accepting the parent's child. Kinship caregivers may also feel guilty about being able to care for the child better than the parent. These feelings can escalate if the child is more attached or responsive to the relative caregiver than to his or her own parents. Kinship caregivers often instruct the children in their care to not refer to them as "Mom" or "Dad" when with their parents.

Embarrassment and guilt may result from the caregiver's reporting or giving of information to agencies that may have a negative impact on the parent's image. Even more embarrassing to the caregiver is the task of explaining to the child why he or she is not with the parent, and how the caregiver may have been involved in the child's relocation (i.e., reporting the parent for abuse/neglect, petitioning for custody or guardianship, obtaining restraining or protection orders).

Kinship caregivers may experience guilt because of their belief that they have betrayed or been disloyal to the parent. These feelings may occur when the relative places the needs of the children before those of the parent.

Finally, embarrassment may arise when the caregiver must request services (i.e., TANF, medical, financial, mental health) from public agencies. Such requests, whether due to the child's special needs or to the caregiver's limited resources, may be in conflict with the caregiver's values and history of independence, self-sufficiency, and privacy.

## Transference and Projection

Transference and projection arise when the kinship caregiver has unresolved issues with the parent that are then transferred or projected to the child. For example, acknowledging a child's resemblance to a parent is usually the highest compliment that can be paid to a child and parent. If the comparisons and resemblance are considered negative, however, then the child is subject to ridicule and misplaced feelings from the caregiver.

Several problems may result from the caregiver's transference and projection. The caregiver may have difficulty perceiving the child's personality as different from that of the parent, the caregiver may not appreciate his or her influence on the child's growth and development (as a role model and primary caregiver), and the caregiver may misinterpret the child's behavior as a personal attack.

## Split/Dual Loyalties

A dilemma many caregivers experience is split and/or dual loyalties to the child and parent. This dilemma arises when the caregiver must place the needs of the child before those of the parent, whom the caregiver may have known first, cared for, or been otherwise attached to. Many kinship caregivers (especially grandparents) have been the recipient of comments from parents such as:

- "How could you report me? I'm your child!"
- "You knew me before you knew my baby."
- "You take better care of the baby than you did me."
- "You'd never let me get away with that."

In situations where the parent is a substance abuser or involved in illegal activity, kinship caregivers may be subjected to comments such as:

- "How can you put me out? I need a place to stay!"
- "You used to always let me stay or come back when I had nowhere to stay, even when I used (drugs)."
- "I'm not using drugs now. Aren't I good enough to be around the kids?"
- "You can let me back. The authorities will never know."

For many caregivers, the fear of or hurt from losing the parent's affection causes the dilemma. Others feel disloyal to the parent because of their unspoken worry: "What will happen to my grown child if I don't continue to help?" Often, thoughts of disloyalty arise when the kinship caregiver feels he or she is usurping the parent's role as the child becomes more attached to the caregiver than to the parent.

## *Anger and Resentment*

Kinship caregivers' anger and resentment may arise from or be directed at the parent, the child, the agency or professionals, or themselves.

Resentment and anger with the parent may be due to the parent's:

- attempts to be reunited with the child, (i.e., in the relative's opinion, the parent is irresponsible);

- freedom from the responsibilities of parenthood;

- failure as a parent;

- embarrassment and hurt to the child or family;

- sabotage of or competition with the caregiver's authority and efforts; or

- efforts to force the relative to "choose" (loyalty) between the child or the parent.

Kinship caregivers may also feel resentment toward the child in their care due to the child's affection, loyalty, and identification with and defense of the parent; desire to return to or maintain contact with the parent; or behavioral problems (i.e., acting out, "ungrateful" attitude). Caregivers may express this resentment verbally: "How could they still love their parents after being abused or neglected?" "Why would they want to be or act like their parents, knowing how they ended up (i.e., addicted, incarcerated)?" "How could they want to return to their parents knowing what they came from or what they are like?" "How could they make excuses for their parents when they know their parents are wrong or irresponsible (i.e., missed visits)?" "How could they misbehave with me? I'm all they have. I didn't abuse or neglect them." "Why don't they appreciate or behave for me? Don't they remember where they came from or what they didn't have?"

Kinship caregivers may also resent or be angry with professionals, community agencies, and institutions for:

- taking the child from the parent if the caregiver feels the removal was unjust;

- allowing the parent to have contact with the child;

- considering the return of the child to the parent;

- competing with or sabotaging the caregiver's authority or role with the child;

- not considering the caregiver's input in placement plans and judicial proceedings;

- not providing adequate supportive services (i.e., funding, legal assistance, day care); or

- having difficult criteria and requirements in order to become eligible for formal or legal caregiver status or for kinship care funding (i.e., guardianship, adoption, foster care status and benefits).

Finally, kinship caregivers are sometimes angry at themselves for deciding to become caregivers. Their anger has its source in their own internal conflicts about the role they have undertaken:

- "I said I wouldn't raise any more children other than my own. Now look at me!"

- "I said I wouldn't take in any more grandchildren or relative children after this one, but I did it again. What's wrong with me?"

- "Somebody's got to take care of the children, but why me? I'm such an idiot."

- "I'm only helping her/him run away from her/his responsibilities. I shouldn't take this child, but I can't let the child go into foster care because of the parent's irresponsibility or my refusal to take the child."

- "I can't believe I'm giving up the rest of my life for these children. I wish I could be selfish like their parents."

## Child-Rearing Practices and Responsibilities

Many kinship caregivers (especially those who are elderly) are challenged by the changes in child-rearing practices that have taken place since they last raised children. What were once considered normal, appropriate, and legal forms of discipline, punishment, and limit setting may now be considered abusive and illegal. Kinship caregivers are confronted with the need to learn noncorporal approaches to disciplining and limit setting (i.e., denying privileges, verbal reprimands, positive and negative reinforcements).

Some kinship caregivers may need to be given an "educational update" on the use of computers, the new math, and so forth if they are to assist the children in their care with homework assignments. Others may be confronting unfamiliar behavioral, emotional, and learning disabilities that may require medication and/or specific behavioral interventions and teaching techniques. These disabilities may range from developmental delays to attention deficit disorder to the symptoms of prenatal alcohol or other drug exposure or the aftereffects of physical or sexual abuse.

Accessing service delivery systems—and ongoing involvement with those systems—is much more complicated for kinship caregivers than for parents in nuclear families. Caregivers who do not have full legal custody of a child may need to negotiate with court systems, child advocates, child welfare systems, and the parents in order to obtain services for the child such as medical treatment, to access subsidized funding, or to enroll the child in school.*

## Morbidity and Mortality

Many kinship caregivers are grandparents, and the potential physical and emotional effects and limitations of aging should not be overlooked. Conceivably, an elderly relative may not live long enough or be physically able to complete the raising of a child, especially a very young child. Thus, kinship caregivers need supportive services and systems in place to compensate for their physical or emotional limitations (i.e., family members, nursing or respite care, medications). Caregivers should develop morbidity and mortality plans to ensure the child's continued care if the caregiver should die or become physically or emotionally incapacitated.

## Overcompensation and Competition

Many kinship caregivers feel extreme empathy and sympathy for the child and parent, given their history (i.e., domestic violence, child neglect/abuse). Consequently, the caregiver may try to "make up" for the child's past losses or traumas, but in doing so, may overcompensate. The task for the caregiver is to provide the child with balance. This task is manageable

---

\*    Chapter Six, "Legal Relationships," examines these concerns in more depth.

once the caregiver realizes that (1) balance and consistency are needed to offset extreme deprivation and instability, and (2) overcompensation only reinforces the child's perception of human behavior and life as "extremes" rather than "balanced."

Part of the balancing process is finding a middle ground between being flexible and being firm, between nurturing and disciplining. Caregivers who may have felt inadequate as parents may try to compensate for their past deficiencies by overindulging the children in their care. This overcompensation is frequently the result of feelings of guilt or responsibility for the parents' problems. Some grandparent caregivers perceive caring for their grandchildren as a "second chance."

Many relatives speak of feeling forced into competition with the parent in order to disprove accusations by the parent about being "unfit" or "no better able to raise a child." Others feel a need to prove to the courts or agencies that they are more qualified than the parent to raise the child. Some want to prove to the child that they are able to provide better care than the child's own parents.

### Fantasies

Many kinship caregivers often express the hope of seeing the parent and child reunited. Such fantasies may become problematic if the caregiver is unable to accept the reality of the parent's needs and limitations. Problems also arise if the caregiver is unable to protect the child from the parent due to fantasies and denial about the parent's limitations and capabilities; if the caregiver is unable to commit to a permanency plan for the child, due to unrealistic fantasies of the child and parent being reunited; or if the caregiver is unable to help the child develop realistic expectations and accept the parent's limitations.

### Redefining Relationships*

The development of a parent/child relationship is facilitated by the child's perception of his or her caregiver as a provider who is protective,

---

* The focus of the discussion in this section is the grandparent/grandchild relationship, since most kinship caregivers are grandparents.

authoritative, and self-sufficient. Nurturance, loyalty, respect, and mutual dependency frequently characterize grandparent/grandchild relationships. The grandparent's age, knowledge, fragility, and position in the family elicits respect from the grandchild. The grandchild's perception of the grandparent as fragile, dependent, and unable to provide for or protect the child, however, prevents the grandchild from perceiving the elderly caregiver as a parent.

To successfully assume a parental role, the caregiver must elicit from the child dependency, confidence, and respect for the caregiver as a provider, protector, and authority figure in a parent/child relationship. Losses, changes, and perhaps some regrets will accompany this development for both the child and the grandparent. The grandparent may lose the role of the unconditionally loyal nurturer—in a disciplinary role, the grandparent may now occasionally be perceived as the "enemy." Because boundaries are much clearer, distance between the child and grandparent may result. These clarified boundaries may also result in a loss of confidential communication that may have once existed between grandchild and grandparent.

Grandparents who take on the raising of their grandchildren must accept that they are now (1) the disciplinarian, (2) independent, and (3) not in need of the child's approval or support. The grandchild in care must give up the role of "little helper." In fact, the grandchild's role may be replaced by other individuals or professionals (i.e., uncles, aunts, nurses, homemakers), clarifying the relationship's boundaries and the grandparent's independence from the child. For example:

> Nine-year-old Tony was reluctant and concerned about moving in with his grandmother. He'd always enjoyed and looked forward to visits and overnights with his grandparent. When asked why he was concerned about living with his grandmother, he explained that he "might kill grandmom. Grandmom says that I make enough noise to wake the dead; and that I might cause her to go to an early grave. Grandmom can only take me for a little time, but I know I should go because grandmom needs my help with shopping and doing things for her."

Several weeks after Tony's grandmother had been informed of his perceptions, his view had changed. His new comments, in somewhat of a resentful and astonished tone, were that "Grandmom doesn't need me the way she used to. She's got nurses and people getting her medicine, cleaning, and even shopping for her. You know grandmom even knows what I'm going to say before I say it, so I can't lie like I used to. She even told me she knows what I'm going to do before I do. She's starting to act like a mom."

## Clinical Issues for the Parent

### *Loss*

Parents who no longer have responsibility for their children may experience the loss of relationships, roles, and purpose, despite their abuse, neglect, or lack of care for those children. In some cases, parents express feelings of having lost the chance "to become a parent," or "to make up for not having been a parent."

Many parents equate the loss of decision-making ability to the loss of authority and control over their children. Even parents who have previously abdicated or delegated the care of their children to relatives or friends for days, weeks, or months at a time find that losing the *option* to take back or give away their children gives rise to separation anxiety and symbolizes the loss of parental rights.

Often, parents experience a loss of status with their child or the kinship caregiver. Parents speak of "losing my child's respect because my child doesn't need me or have to listen to me anymore." Many fear losing their child's respect and dependency to whomever is the caregiver or authority figure (i.e., relative, case worker).

To many parents, having a child has earned them the status of adulthood in the family. To lose the role of parenthood is to lose equal status and respect within the family system and hierarchy. Parents often feel the loss of this equal status, particularly if the kinship caregiver is their parent or sibling. The parent may say that he or she feels like a child or feels controlled by the kinship caregiver through the child, as the caregiver can determine when, how long, and where the parent can visit. The caregiver may know more about the child's needs than the parent and may instruct the parent about the child's care (i.e., times for meals, medication, bedtime, attire).

Parents also may experience a loss of respect and trust from the children who remain with them. Remaining children may either verbally or nonverbally communicate disapproval with their parent for "losing" or "giving up" their sibling. Fears of "Will I be the next to go?" impact the children's trust in their parents' ability to keep or care for them.

### Role and Boundary Redefinition

The reassignment of parental responsibilities when a child is placed in kinship care causes a redefinition of and shift in roles and boundaries. These shifts create much of the confusion and tension between relatives, children, and parents. Parents may find that their role has changed from primary caregiver to supporter, from nurturer to consoling friend, from decision maker to advisor, or from authority/parental figure to family relative.

Parents frequently have difficulty relinquishing their roles to kinship caregivers. They may need assistance in helping their children accept the shift in roles and boundaries, in not competing with the kinship caregivers, and in not sabotaging the child's acceptance of the caregiver due to unresolved parental jealousy, anger, fantasies, or losses.

As the roles and boundaries between the parent and the kinship caregiver change, the parent, no longer in charge of the child, must

- support the relative's parental role;

- make suggestions to rather than direct the relative about the child's care;

- accept the relative's actions and decisions as final;

- request the relative's approval or permission regarding activities with the child; and

- refer the child to the kinship caregiver for limit setting, discipline, instruction, permission, or nurturance.

## *Guilt*

Parental guilt arises from feelings of failure, disappointment, and embarrassment about the child living with a relative while family members' and friends' children still live with their parents, or about professionals and agencies providing family preservation and reunification services. This guilt will occur and reoccur as the parent works through the different phases of the grief and loss process. Consequently, the parent may, at different points in time:

- deny any guilt feelings;

- present a pseudoacceptance of the child's placement with relatives as in the child's best interest;

- displace blame for the child's placement onto relatives, the case worker, agencies, or the court;

- abdicate future responsibility for or contact with the child (i.e., "My child will be better off without me"); or

- express hopelessness about ever getting or deserving the child's return or affection.

The parent's guilt and low self-esteem may be strong enough to prevent him or her from resuming parental responsibilities and care for the child, especially if the placement was due to the parent's substance abuse, criminal behavior or incarceration, psychiatric history, or HIV infection. Sometimes, a parent may conceive another child to "replace" the child in kinship care. This may cause further guilt, however, as the parent knows that there is already a child waiting to return home.

## *Anger*

Parental anger may be directed at or arise from several sources, including (1) the agencies, professionals and courts; (2) the kinship caregiver; and (3) the child. Parents may also be angry with themselves.

Anger with agencies and the professional community may be due to the parent's feelings and opinions about:

- the child being given to relatives;

- agencies and courts making unrealistic expectations and demands of the parent as a prerequisite to regaining or keeping the child (i.e., tasks, timetables);

- unavailable or inaccessible services;

- insensitive or nonsupportive professionals;

- the lack of adequate legal representation;

- the system and courts being influenced by vindictive relatives; or

- jealousy of the professional's relationship with the child and relatives.

The parent's anger with the kinship caregiver may be due to:

- the kinship caregiver's acceptance of the child in his or her home (i.e., "If you hadn't accepted my child, the court would have left the child with me; you gave them an alternative to me");

- the kinship caregiver having reporting the parent to an agency (i.e., for abuse, neglect);

- the kinship caregiver's attempts to not have the child returned to the parent;

- the kinship caregiver's success with the child (i.e., health, school performance, behavior);

- jealousy of the kinship caregiver's relationship with and attachment to the child; or

- feelings that the kinship caregiver is undermining the parent's role and relationship with the child (i.e., verbally demeaning the parent, buying the child's loyalty and affection with toys, "spoiling" the child).

The parent's anger with the child may be due to:

- the child's attachment to the caregiver (perceived by the parent as disloyalty);

- the child's disclosure of events that may have occurred while living with the parent (perceived by the parent as betrayal);

- the child's acceptance of the caregiver as an authority figure and nurturer;

- the child's ability to excel and flourish while living in kinship care (i.e., improved school performance, health, social skills) (perceived as embarrassing); or

- the child's appearing happier to be with relatives than with the parent (perceived as rejection).

## Disloyalty and Rejection

Many parents may have had codependent relationships with the kinship caregiver or the caregiver may have had a history of "rescuing" or "enabling" the parent. Some relatives may even have allowed themselves to be abused (verbally or physically) or otherwise victimized (property or money stolen) by the parent. When relatives assume responsibility for a child, the parent may feel abandoned by the relative and replaced by the child or jealous of or in competition with the child for the relative's loyalty. The parent may believe that the child is more important to the relative than the parent is or that the child's needs supersede those of the parent. Frequently, the parent's perception is that the kinship caregiver is giving better care and more attention to the child than he or she gave to the parent prior to the child's arrival, or is more permissive with the child than with the parent (i.e., "You never let me get away with that"). The parent may also feel that the caregiver is siding with the child against the parent (i.e., reporting the parent for abuse or neglect, filing for custody, restraining orders, or criminal complaints).

## Projection and Transference

The parent's projection and transference appear to originate from three sources: (1) unresolved past issues with the kinship caregiver and/or child; (2) unresolved guilt and low self-esteem; or (3) suspicions and mistrust of other's opinions and loyalty.

The placement of a child in care often elicits feelings of guilt and inadequacy from the parent. Consequently, the parent may assume that others will also perceive him or her as inadequate and a failure. Unfortunately, such projections can cause the parent to become distrustful and defensive with kinship caregivers, professionals, and the child.

The parent's unresolved issues with the kinship caregiver further complicates their relationship. The parent may challenge the child-rearing practices of the kinship caregiver in an effort to protect the child from experiences the parent had during childhood or adolescence, saying:

- "I'm not going to let you make the same mistakes with my child as you did with me."

- "You're already starting to affect my child the same way you affected me."

- "You're trying to make my child think like you so you can turn him/her against me."

- "My child didn't start acting like this toward me until she started living with you."

Such perceptions become problematic when the parent is unaware that the child is becoming an extension of unresolved issues that the parent has with the caregiver.

## Sabotage and Competition

Sabotage is frequently a result of the parent's anger, projection, transference, feelings of abandonment, and disloyalty. The parent may sabotage the placement by undermining the caregiver's or agency's authority or by triangulating the child.

Consciously and unconsciously, many parents will test or undermine the authority of the relative caregiver, courts, agency, or professional. The parent may challenge, defy, or not comply with instructions or directives such as curfews and visiting procedures. In some instances, parents have reported caregivers and professionals for abuse, neglect, or inappropriate behavior.

The parent may also triangulate the child by:

- giving the child permission to defy caregivers, agencies, and professionals;

- causing the child to feel guilty or disloyal for complying with anyone other than the parent;

- verbally demeaning and degrading those in authority in the presence of the child; or

- colluding with the child's feelings of discontent, mistreatment, defiance, or fantasy of returning to the parent.

The parent's triangulation of the child can be unconscious or conscious; deliberate or unintentional. The child's loyalty and enmeshment with the parents may result in acting-out behavior, however, if the parent is in denial or unable to maintain clear boundaries and expectations.

### Fantasy Issues

Many parents fantasize that they will soon be reunited with their children. Such fantasies become a problem when they are unobtainable and unrealistic. They may cause the child to maintain unrealistic fantasies of reuniting with the parent, cause difficulty for the kinship caregiver in engaging in a permanency plan for the child, or result in the parent sabotaging any attempts to stabilize the child's behavior or permanent living arrangements.

Parental fantasies may have several causes:

- The parent may be in the denial phase of the loss and grief process.

- The parent may be avoiding the consequences and feelings associated with failures and mistakes.

- The parent may be attempting to maintain an image of being a "good parent" for friends, family members, and the child.

- The parent may be under pressure from professionals, relatives, and friends because of the latter's fantasies or guilt (i.e., "If the parent fails, then we have also failed").

- The parent may be avoiding the feeling of "I gave up fighting," which could mean "I gave up fighting for my children."

- The parent may need to feel a sense of choice or control, even if the only sense of choice is the choice to resist giving up the fantasy (or hope).

- The parent may be under pressure from siblings who may still reside with the parent.

## Clinical Issues for the Child

### Loss

The most obvious loss in kinship care is the child's loss of the parents. Often, children believe that it is better to have an abusive or absent parent than to "not have any parent at all." Whether their feelings are real or imagined, many children express a loss of love or of a special relationship with their parents.

Children also feel the loss of their siblings. In fact, the loss of a parentified sibling may be felt as deeply as the loss of a parent. Many children may tolerate the loss of their parents well provided they remain with their siblings in placement.

Children placed into care experience a loss of privacy and space, as well as the loss of a home of their own. They may feel like an intruder or boarder in the kinship caregiver's home, or miss a sense of family ownership, no matter how transient or deplorable their former living conditions may have been.

The loss of normalcy is also verbalized by some children, who may state: "I wish I lived with my parents like other children" or "I wish I had normal parents like other children." Sometimes, kinship caregivers report hearing the children fabricate stories for other children about why they are living with their relatives (i.e., "My parents are in the hospital," or "My dad is in the service," or "My mom is working in another city").

Children in kinship care may feel the loss of rights, privileges, and entitlements. When living with their parents and siblings, children know their place in the family hierarchy by both birthright and rites of passage. Children in kinship care, however, often speak of feeling like Cinderella, or of being an intruder or burden. Consequently, these children may feel indebted rather than entitled to live with their relatives, feelings they may have never experienced as their relative's guest or visitor, when they had parents and a home to which they could return.

Another loss for the child arises from the change in the relationship with the kinship caregiver, especially if the caregiver is a grandparent. Before placement into kinship care, the child may have viewed the relative as unconditionally loyal and forgiving, a private confident, or a friend, not a disciplinarian. The child may have turned to the relative for occasional protection from the parent, or may have developed a mutually dependent relationship because of the relative's fragility or age. When the relative becomes a parental figure, however, the child may lose this relationship. Unconditional friends become limit setters; former "protectors" become the "enemy." Children often describe their relatives' metamorphosis as "they changed-up" or "they're acting like parents."

The change in relationships with their other relatives represents an additional loss for children in kinship care. Cousins may become jealous of the child who has full access to and lives with the grandparent. Grandparents, for their part, may now treat the child as their own child by birth instead of as another grandchild. Children who live with a grandparent may also feel jealousy and resentment from aunts and uncles (the grandparent's adult children). Many children report hearing aunts and uncles saying, "Mom, you never let us get away with the things you let this grandchild get away with" or "Mom, you're too elderly to keep up with this child; my brother (or sister) had no right to leave their child with you." Children who personalize their relatives' jealousy and resentment experience a loss of closeness or acceptance by other family members.

## Rejection and Abandonment

Children in care frequently try to justify and rationalize why their parents couldn't keep or properly care for them. Feelings of rejection and abandonment, however, may still be subconsciously prevalent or simply denied:

During a therapy session, 11-year-old Jerry was explaining why his father allowed him to be placed with his grandmother. Jerry explained that: (1) his dad didn't have enough money, (2) they had been "put out" by the landlord, and (3) his dad couldn't find a job. The child withheld information he knew about his father's drug use and arrest as reasons for his father's lack of money and employment.

When asked if there were any reasons or circumstances that would make him place his child when he became a parent, Jerry responded, "No." When asked why not, he stated, "I wouldn't want my child to be mad at me for giving him away or to think I didn't loved him."

When asked if that is how he felt about his dad, Jerry quickly responded, "No, my daddy loves me. He had to give me to my grandmother until things get better."

When Jerry pretended to be a parent, he did not give himself the same excuses and understanding he gave his father. Once Jerry realized that the child he was pretending to be was accusing his father of abandonment and rejection, he quickly began to rejustify his father's behavior.

## Guilt and Low Self-Esteem

Children may experience guilt and low self-esteem if they internalize responsibility for causing their parents to place them with relatives, perceive themselves as burdens to their parents (and now their kinship caregiver), or feel inferior to children, relatives, and siblings who are not in care.

Loyalty to their parents prevents children from holding their parents responsible for problems and the placement. Children have been known to state that they deserved to be abused, neglected, and abandoned by their parents. Thus, it is common to hear these children accept responsibility for being victimized (i.e., "I asked for it," or "Everybody would be better off without me," or "They wouldn't have these problems if I wasn't around"). Many of these statements reflect comments the children hear from their parents.

Guilt and low self-esteem can be further escalated if the child maintains these same attitudes when placed with a kinship caregiver. Consequently, the child will be predisposed to feeling that he or she is a burden to the caregiver. In the past, the child may have always felt like a guest, entitled to visit or stay with a relative. Now, however, the child may feel indebted because of the lack of parents or a home to which he or she can return.

Feeling inferior to or different from other children may also be a source of low self-esteem for children in kinship care. They may feel that their lifestyles and living arrangements are abnormal. A frequent comment by children in kinship families is "most children live with at least one parent." Some children seem to find living with divorced or separated parents more socially acceptable than living with relatives.

## Anger and Resentment

The child's anger and resentment may arise from, or be directed at, the parent, relative caregiver, or agency, court system, or professionals.

Children may be angry with their parents for:

- allowing themselves to be put in a situation that resulted in the child's placement;

- taking advantage of relatives by giving them additional children and responsibilities;

- choosing "to give them away" instead of another sibling;

- choosing to conceive additional children while the child is still in placement;

- continuing to have the same problems that resulted in the child's initial placement (i.e., drugs, unemployment, eviction, incarceration) and thus failing to regain custody;

- parental conflicts with the kinship caregiver;

- not keeping visits, contact, or promises; or

- the parent's lifestyle, (i.e., drugs, incarceration, HIV, homelessness), which causes embarrassment for the child.

The child may also be angry with the parent for agreeing to voluntarily place him or her. Involuntary placement is sometimes more acceptable to children, who rationalize that "at least my parents didn't give me up without a fight." Voluntary placement suggests to a child that "I wasn't worth fighting for" or "My parents didn't even want to keep me."

The child may be angry with or resent the kinship caregiver for agreeing to the placement, reasoning that, "If you hadn't taken me then I'd still be with my parents. He or she may resent the caregiver for petitioning for custody or guardianship or for taking legal action against the parent (i.e., obtaining a restraining order, reporting abuse).

The child may defy and resist the caregiver's authority if the caregiver was more of a friend or peer prior to the placement, such as in a grandparent/grandchild relationship. Anger and resentment may also arise if the child is acting out the parent's anger or unresolved issues (i.e., triangulating) with the relative or reacting to the relative's transference and projection of unresolved issues with the parent (i.e., "You're just like your parents, but I'll straighten you out"). The child may also be displacing onto the caregiver anger with the parent or from past trauma. Finally, anger toward the caregiver may be due to the generation gap and values conflict between the child and relative.

Anger with agencies, court systems, and professionals may be due to:

- the agency's removal of the child from the home;

- the agency or court's termination of the parent's rights;

- the child acting out the relative's or parent's anger;

- the professional having an authoritative role with the child;

- the agency or professional taking legal action against the parent (i.e., reporting abuse, terminating visits);

- the agency or professional encouraging the relative caregiver to petition for legal status or to pursue legal action; or

- the agency or court pursuing a parent/child reunification plan against the child's wishes.

## *Split Loyalty*

The child may experience divided loyalties among the kinship caregiver, the parent, siblings, and professionals. These divided loyalties become a problem for the child when the recipients of the child's loyalty are in competition with each other; the child's divided loyalties are interpreted by the recipient as *dis*loyalty; the child is given the ultimatum to choose between loved ones or risk rejection; or the child is manipulated or triangulated by individuals to whom the child is loyal.

Loyalty to the parent arises from:

- past attachments, bonding, and nurturing experiences (imagined or real);

- role reversal (in which the child became parentified and nurtured the parent);

- fantasies of how deserving the parent is of loyalty;

- fear of being rejected by the parent if not totally loyal;

- pity and a desire to avoid abandoning the parent;

- defiance of those who feel the parent is undeserving of loyalty;

- developmental issues associated with role models and identification with the parent; or

- fear of hurting the parents' feelings.

The child's past attachments to and experiences with the caregiver prior to the placement may inspire loyalty, as will the quality of care and bonding since the placement. The child may feel a need to compensate for the parent's animosity or disloyalty toward the relative caregiver, or may feel indebted to the relative, fear abandonment or rejection, or fear hurting the relative's feelings.

The child's loyalty to his or her siblings may be due to training throughout childhood to have a strong allegiance to one's brothers and sisters. In the absence of adult parental figures, sibling relationships may also become parentified, that is, the siblings take on the role and responsibility of parenting. Finally, loyalty to siblings may be due to the child's desire to reaffirm the siblings' identity as a family while living separately from each other and the parents.

The child's loyalty to the professional may result from the professional "being there" in times of crisis and having the power and authority to protect and remove the child from harmful situations. The professional who follows through with promises and commitments also may earn the child's loyalty, as will those professionals whom the child sees as being directed by "the child's best interest."

## Embarrassment

A major source of embarrassment for the child in kinship care is the discovery by others that the child is not being raised by his or her parents. As the goal of the child is not to be discovered, any visible evidence indicating that the caregiver is not the parent is embarrassing to the child. Possibly the two most embarrassing situations for children in kinship care are (1) when the age difference between themselves and their caregivers is visible, extreme, and obvious; and (2) when the relative caregiver is unable to publicly participate with them in normal parent/child activities (i.e., father/son sports events, father/daughter dance contests).

## Projection and Transference

Children are vulnerable to projecting their own fears, biases, and misperceptions onto others if they are unaware of their own insecurities and fears. They may mistrust the abilities of others to form unbiased or objective opinions about them or may be prejudiced or biased toward caregivers based on the influence of other's opinions or prejudices. These conditions can cause obstacles between the child and the caregiver. The child's projections are frequently evidenced in statements such as "I can tell by how she looks at me that this won't work," or "See how she talks to me; my dad told me to be ready for that."

The obstacles may increase if the child transfers roles and characteristics to the relative from unresolved experiences or trauma with previous adults. The child may believe that "All adults use kids" or "Those closest to you hurt you, especially parents." Unfortunately the child may be unable to perceive the caregiver as a separate person with his or her own individual personality, strengths, and limits. Instead, the caregiver becomes an extension of other adults and the child's memories.

## *Sabotage*

Relative placements are as easily subject to disruptions by children as nonrelative placements. The child's attempt to sabotage the placement may be due to the child's demonstration of loyalty to the parent, the child's attempt to keep the parent involved, the child acting out the parent's unresolved issues, or the child acting out his or her own projections and fantasies.

Children may feel they are demonstrating loyalty to their parents by attempting to disrupt the placement. They perceive cooperation with the caregiver as disloyalty to their parents. They may also fear embarrassing their parents by being more responsive to the caregiver than they were to the parents.

Some children sabotage their placement out of fear of losing contact with their parents. They believe that if they act out, their parents will have to intervene and "make them behave." They may have developed a pattern of getting attention when misbehaving, and continue to believe that the only way to get their parents' attention is to create a crisis. If they cooperate with their relatives, then their parents may not feel needed or remain in contact.

Children may also be hopeful that acting out may result in their return to their parents. They may believe that they have their parents' nonverbal permission to initiate such a plan because of a shared fantasy of reunification. Such misbehavior is reinforced if the children observe their parents degrading the caregiver or belittling the agency or professionals.

In some instances, the child's projections and transferences may sabotage several placements. The child's assumption that the placement "won't work" discourages any real attempt to cooperate with professionals, agencies, or kinship caregivers.

## Redefining Boundaries and Relationships

One of the most difficult tasks for the child is to accept the exchange of roles between the kinship caregiver and the parent. The child must adjust to seeing the relative as the primary caregiver, decision maker, authority figure, and disciplinarian, and the parent as a supporter or advisor.

Kinship caregivers, in their parental role, must establish boundaries that may not have existed prior to the child's placement. For their part, parents must defer to the authoritative role of relatives as primary caregivers. Consequently, the child must relate to the relative as a parent and to the parent as a supportive relative. The child's initial confusion escalates if either the parent or the caregiver does not accept the change in roles.

Several behaviors and attitudes can be anticipated from the child during the redefinition of roles and boundaries:

- testing, defying, and resenting the caregiver's authority;

- feeling as though the parent should have authority;

- resenting the caregiver having authority over the parent's involvement;

- encouraging the parent to defy the caregiver's authority and control;

- becoming angry with the parent for accepting the caregiver's authority;

- complaining to the parent or professional about the caregiver's misuse or abuse of authority (i.e., child abuse reports); and

- manipulating and attempting to split the caregiver and parent, especially if the adults are in conflict about the changes in their roles.

These behaviors and attitudes may occur in reverse when the parent tries to resume the parental role during reunification efforts or visits, if the child is resistant to separating from the kinship caregiver.

## *Morbidity and Mortality*

The child in kinship care is often concerned with issues of illness and death. These concerns may be triggered by previous losses and separations, the kinship caregiver's age and medical conditions associated with aging; the parent's high-risk lifestyle (i.e., substance abuse, incarceration), or the child's codependency or pseudoadult relationship with the parent or caregiver. Children with mortality and morbidity concerns may question:

- Who will take care of my mom or dad if I'm not there?

- Who will take care of grandma and grandpa if they get sick?

- Who is going to take care of me if everyone gets sick or dies?

# Chapter Three
# *Assessment and Intervention*

## A Family and Systems Approach

Professionals working with kinship families should consider adopting a family approach and systems model, which provide a framework for practice that is: (1) family and systems oriented; (2) interagency and interdisciplinary; (3) interactive with clients and consumers; (4) both short and long term; and (5) developmental in response to the stages and cycles of individuals, families, and organizations.

A family approach interprets each family member's behavior and problems as a function of the family system. The approach facilitates the creation of genograms and an understanding of family dyads and triads; allows examination of multiple households as well as permanent and transient household (family) members and caregivers (related and nonrelated), and accommodates the use of various family therapy models and approaches (i.e., structural, contextual, strategic) to address nuclear, extended, intergenerational, and cultural family dynamics.

A systems model identifies points of intervention on a micro and macro level. On a micro level, the child and the family can receive separate or integrated interventions (i.e., individual and family therapy and services). On the macro level, systems model strategies help families become self-sufficient and function independently in meeting the needs of their members. Macro-level strategies include the development of services, programs, and policies that support a family's ecology (i.e., neighborhood, community, health, housing, employment).

Combining a family approach and systems model minimizes the fragmentation of interventions and the isolated interpretation of problems. Goals and strategies are established that are complimentary and comprehensive. Questions of "Who is the client?" and "Where do we begin?" are more manageable and less overwhelming. The needs of individuals, families, agencies and communities can be identified, and intermittent or simultaneous services or modifications provided.

## Assessing a Family for Kinship Care

Children may live with kinship caregivers either formally or informally. Frequently, the family's culture and legacies determine the child's status. In many instances, the child is initially placed informally; later, the placement may be legally formalized through foster care, guardianship, custody, or adoption proceedings.

In assessing a caregiver's ability to raise a relative's child, professionals must examine the caregiver's motivation, the status of other household residents, caregiver/parent interactions, family legacies, child-rearing practices, material resources, and alternative permanency plans.

### *Motivation*

What motivates a person to raise a relative's child? While each caregiver's reasons differ, such decisions usually are motivated by feelings of loyalty, attachment, obligation, penance, rescuing, or anger.

Many relatives are driven by loyalty, either to the family, parent, or child. Loyalty to a family tradition or a legacy of being self-sufficient and independent may motivate some caregivers, who may state: "We take care of our own," or "Our family always sticks together," or "None of our children have or will ever go into placement."

For many caregivers, the loyalty that motivates them may be to a fantasy that the parent will at a later time assume responsibility for the child. To not keep or accept the child would make the caregiver feel guilty and disloyal to the parent or family.

In some situations, the child may have already been sharing the same home with the caregiver, but as a member of a separate household (i.e., in a home with multiple households or multigenerational families). Consequently, the caregiver may have developed a relationship with the parent and child by having been a secondary caregiver or in-home neighbor. Loyalty to these existing relationships motivates the relative to become a caregiver.

Relatives who have served as secondary caregivers may be motivated by attachment to become kinship caregivers. Such attachments often originate when a relative lives in close proximity to the child. In some instances, the relative may occasionally have been the child's primary caregiver due to the parent's circumstances (i.e., illness, unemployment, marital problems, work schedule, substance abuse, incarceration). Relatives' comments often provide a clue to this motivation: "I've been baby-sitting this child since her birth." "We've lived together for years in the same home, we're just like family." "The child has been with me since he was an infant, I feel like a parent to him."

In some instances, the caregiver feels obligated to accept or keep a relative's child by "default" due to the lack of alternative caregivers, reasoning that "someone has to do it." The caregiver may feel trapped or forced by responsibility, tradition, or other commitments to care for the child. Although the caregiver may also have feelings of loyalty or attachment to the child, these feelings alone would not motivate the relative to pursue or keep the child "if someone else would do it."

Penance can be a strong motivating factor. Some caregivers gladly accept caring for a child as a second chance to atone for past mistakes and guilt. They may feel that they are atoning for their own children having been raised by other family members or feel responsible for the parent's inability to keep the child (i.e., if the caregiver had been an absent parent to the parent). Some may look on their caregiving as atoning to friends and family for the parent's mistakes or absence.

Some caregivers are motivated by a belief that they are "rescuing" the child from:

- abuse or neglect by the parent;

- exposure to immoral lifestyles (i.e., drugs, prostitution, criminal behavior) or inappropriate role models;

- unsupervised, unstructured, and understimulating environments;

- inappropriate extended family members (i.e., mother or father; maternal or paternal extended family); or

- community agencies and institutions (i.e., nonrelative foster care, courts, professionals).

Some caregivers are motivated to take on the care of a child by their anger with the parent or agency. Anger with the parent may originate in unresolved issues with the parent prior to the child's birth, disappointment or embarrassment caused by the parent, the parent's unwillingness to accept the relative's advice or help, or the parent's denying the child contact with relatives.

Anger with community agencies and institutions may be due to the agency's attempts to reunify or preserve the parent/child relationship and contacts. The caregiver may also be angry with the agency for not removing the child from the parent in response to the caregiver's concerns or allegations against the parent.

## Household Residents

Many household configurations include multigenerational families and multiple households (related and/or nonrelated), where families and households share not only a home, but also child care and child-rearing responsibilities. Such configurations may develop out of necessity, culture, or convenience. Children in such households are exposed to a variety of adult models, child-rearing practices, limits, styles of nurturing, family legacies, and patterns of interaction. As exposure may vary among family members and generations, as well as between households, each separate household's residents—as well as the caregiver's immediate family— must be assessed. The assessment of household and individual residents should examine permanent, temporary, or transient households (related and nonrelated), and include permanent, temporary, or transient individuals and members of the family (related and nonrelated).

Patterns of residency and transiency among households and their members must be considered since many families have cycles in which members and households exit, reenter, and re-exit (i.e., after college, divorces, drug rehabilitation, incarceration, hospitalization, marriages).

## Caregivers

Many cultures (i.e., Asian, Latino, African American) include nonrelatives in their immediate or extended families. Children residing in multiple households or with multigenerational families may have both primary and secondary caregivers. An assessment of all potential caregivers is essential in determining the extent to which a child may be exposed to care that is contradictory, inconsistent, unstable, or threatening (physically or emotionally). All potential caregivers, whether or not they are related, should undergo background checks as well. A standardized background check, as in any home study, should include medical, criminal, educational, employment, substance abuse, and psychiatric histories.

## Parental Involvement with the Kinship Family

Assessing the parent's involvement with the kinship family is essential for determining the emotional stability of the child's environment, as well as for determining the caregiver's ability to stabilize the child's environment and comply with any legal conditions related to the parent's involvement. If plans call for the parent to have contact with the child (i.e., visiting), the professional assessing the placement should ask:

- Is the caregiver able to comply with any legal stipulation determining the parent's involvement (or restricted involvement), regardless of his or her personal feelings?

- Is the caregiver able to avoid triangulating the child (i.e., encourage or discourage the child's involvement with the parent)?

- How will the caregiver restrict or allow the parent's involvement (i.e., decision making, disciplining, nurturing activities)?

- What is the quality of the caregiver/parent relationship (past and present)?

- What is the potential for the caregiver and parent to resolve past or present issues and renegotiate parental roles?

- How will the caregiver allow the parent's extended family to be involved with the child?

The last question must be asked because of the child's possible attachment (or past or future involvement) with the maternal or paternal extended family. For example:

> A child placed with his paternal grandparents previously lived with his mother and maternal grandparents. The child's emotional stability required contact with the maternal grandparents, but contact with the mother was legally prohibited. The situation was further complicated because the mother was a transient family member in the maternal grandparents' home due to her drug use.

> Should the caregiver allow the child to continue contact with the extended family? How? Where? When?

Ideally, the assessment should include the parent and extended family in determining how to involve relatives and parents in meeting the child's emotional needs. The questions previously listed should be asked of the parent and extended family members as well, with respect to their interaction with the kinship caregiver.

## Family Legacies, Cycles, and Patterns

The assessment must also consider the caregiver's ability to interrupt the child's exposure to or repetition of the family's cycles and patterns. The professional should identify and assess the family's legacies (behaviors and problems experienced or handed down by predecessors); the family's life cycles; the family's child-rearing patterns, structures, and practices; and the caregiver's and family's potential to change and alter their life cycles, patterns, and legacies.

Problems and behaviors for consideration as legacies include patterns or histories of substance abuse, child abuse, domestic violence, incarceration, education, employment, and socioeconomic status.

Life cycle issues for assessment include:

- When do adult members date, become single couples, or engage in preparing for a family (i.e., nesting), if at all?

- How quickly do children experience developmental stages, if at all (i.e., missed childhood)?

- At what age and how do family members exit or reenter the family system (i.e., teenage runaway; exit via marriage, college, or pregnancy; reentry following marital separation, drug rehabilitation, incarceration, college, or military service)?

- What life cycles are missed or difficult to negotiate as individuals and as a family?

The assessment of family child-rearing practices, patterns, and structures should include:

- the family configuration in which the child is raised (i.e., nuclear, multigenerational, family, multiple household);

- approaches to limit setting and disciplining (i.e., corporal versus noncorporal punishment, verbal reprimands, denying privileges, positive reinforcement);

- family and child-rearing goals (dependence, independence, or interdependence of individuals or family members); and

- child-rearing patterns (role reversal, pseudoadult children, parentified sibling systems).

The assessment of the family's ability to change and alter legacies should include examination of the caregiver's personal repetition or interruption of legacies during his or her own life cycle; the family's motivation to change; the availability of resources and supports to inspire and stabilize the family's change; and the caregiver's ability to limit the child's exposure to legacies and child-rearing practices of other family members or households in the caregiver's home.

## *Family Resources*

Standardized home studies are frequently used to assess a family's ability to meet the material, medical, and educational needs of a child. The standards may vary depending on whether the kinship family is pursuing status as a foster family or as an adoptive family.

Emphasis should be placed on helping families meet the criteria used in home studies. Some agencies are developing standards specific for kinship families. The challenge they face, however, is to avoid developing criteria that are substandard in an effort to keep children with their kinship families, while not creating standards that are too rigid for families to meet.

## *Alternative Permanency Plans*

When assessing kinship caregivers who are grandparents, issues of morbidity and mortality associated with aging must be considered. The caregiver's plan for continuation of the child's care in his or her absence should be assessed.

Caregivers usually rely on commitments and promises from other family members. During the assessment, verification of these commitments should be obtained through copies of wills, letters of agreement, or interviews with family members.

The professional should also assess respite plans. Depending on the caregiver's age and health, supports may be needed to temporarily relieve the caregiver of parental responsibilities and activities. Interviews with family or friends to verify their availability may be required. Observation of the plan's implementation, both during and after the assessment process, would be most validating.

## Intervention Strategies with Kinship Families

Using a systems approach and family therapy model, strategies for intervening with kinship families, as well as goals, methods, and points of intervention, can be identified. The points of intervention in the discussion that follows include the dyads and triads that exist in the kinship family system.* The dyads discussed include the kinship caregiver/child; the kinship caregiver/parent; the kinship caregiver/professional; the child/parent; the child/siblings; the child/professional; and the professional/parent. Individual intervention with the caregiver, child, and parent may be a prerequisite to or occur simultaneously with dyad and triad interventions.

## Points of Intervention

### Caregiver/Child Dyad

The official placement of a child by an agency sometimes evokes family dynamics that did not exist when the child and parent shared a home with the relative, or when the child was informally placed with the relative, with the parent's knowledge or consent. In some instances, the child, parent, and kinship caregiver may have been living together as a multiple or intergenerational household. Once a child is "moved" from one household to another, however, clinical issues of kinship care arise and the family must be viewed as a "blended" family, even though no physical change in living arrangements may have taken place.

Clinical issues and goals for the kinship caregiver and child include:

- defining rules, mutual expectations, routines, schedules, discipline, consequences, rewards, and other structural family issues;

- engaging the caregiver and child in a loss and grief process related to changes and losses in their own relationship (i.e., the change from a peer, friend, or codependent relationship to a parent/child relationship);

- engaging in a loss and grief process related to the parent;

- establishing methods of testing and earning trust, loyalty, and mutual respect;

---

* Intervention strategies with individual family members are addressed within the context of a systems approach and model.

- engaging in a bonding process using testing, common losses, grief, and quality time together;

- minimizing the projection and transference that may occur between the caregiver and the child; and

- redefining the relationships and activities with the parent and with the child's immediate and extended family (i.e., siblings, maternal or paternal extended family).

### Caregiver / Parent Dyad

The caregiver and the parent will need to interact as a dyad, whether or not they have a history of conflict or unresolved issues, to minimize and manage the child's confusion, manipulation, or resistance to the placement, changes, and differences in the households.

Clinical goals and issues for the kinship caregiver and parent include:

- redefining roles, interactions, and activities with each other and with the child;

- identifying methods of decision making, conflict resolution, and problem solving that do not triangulate the child;

- identifying and minimizing each other's projections and transference resulting from unresolved issues or current conflicts;

- identifying and deescalating each other's competition or sabotage;

- engaging in sharing and "reality testing" mutual fantasies;

- engaging in a loss and grief process related to their relationship and the child; and

- establishing goals for the child and joint methods for accomplishing them (i.e., education, health, psychosocial development).

### Caregiver / Professional Dyad

The professional must be considered part of the family's system because of the professional's authority and ability to affect decisions, family interactions, and roles. Family members may perceive the professional (and the agency the professional represents) as a source of competition or as an ally. Issues of fantasy, protection, or sabotage often come into play. On the one hand, the professional is vulnerable to being triangulated; on the other, the professional can be instrumental in stabilizing the family's dynamics.

Goals and issues for the kinship caregiver and professional include:

- clarifying each other's roles, relationship, and authority with the child and parent (i.e., housing, education, and health decisions; discipline; visiting and parental contact with the child);

- clarifying the agency's and professional's role and authority with the caregiver;

- identifying and minimizing the caregiver's projections and transferences resulting from unresolved issues or conflicts with previous agencies and professionals;

- identifying a method of conflict resolution, decision making, and problem solving that will prevent the professional from being triangulated by the child or parent;

- developing methods to avoid competition, sabotage, and the undermining of each other's roles and authority;

- identifying appropriate roles and involvement of the parent with the caregiver (i.e., shared disciplining, nurturing, decision making);

- engaging the caregiver in reality testing his or her own fantasies, as well as resolving loss, grief, and guilt issues; and

- developing structure for the child (i.e., rules, expectations, consequences, reward systems, disciplinary techniques).

### Child/Parent Dyad

The child's real or imagined loyalty and attachment to, or anger with, the parent makes their interaction as a dyad necessary, whether or not the parent has been present in the child's life as a parental figure.

Goals and issues for the child and parent include:

- the parent's identification of new roles, relationships, and authority with the child;

- the parent's identification and support of the caregiver's roles and authority;

- the parent giving permission to the child to attach to, be loyal to, and cooperate with the caregiver;

- the parent's incorporation of the caregiver's rules, discipline, and expectations during contacts and visits with the child (i.e., curfews, dress codes, consequences);

- deescalating any collusion with the child to compete with, sabotage, or undermine the caregiver's authority or image;

- allowing the child to express anger or hurt about the placement or with the parent (as part of the child's loss and grief process);

- the parent's acceptance of responsibility for not being able to care for the child (if applicable);

- exonerating the child of any guilt, blame, or responsibility for the placement;

- allowing the child to address any past trauma or memories of unresolved issues from the past involving the parent, to minimize displaced anger or transference (i.e., past abuse or neglect by the parent);

- promoting acceptance of responsibility for past events, when appropriate; and

- discouraging the child's unrealistic fantasies (i.e., return to parent or family).

## Child/Sibling Dyad

Whether siblings are placed together with a relative or placed in separate homes, the child/sibling dyad cannot be ignored. Children from parentified sibling groups may be in special need of therapeutic contact with each other in order to accept their kinship families and separation.

Goals and issues for siblings include:

- helping the children to acknowledge each other's right to a family, give each other permission to attach to and become members of other families, identify how they will remain in contact with each other, acknowledge each other's loss and grief, and exonerate each other of any disloyalty or blame for not staying together, especially if they promised each other or their parents that they would stay together and take care of each other;

- determining how they will maintain their identity as a family (i.e., keep last name, visit, phone); and

- helping the child in care to "become a child" and allow adults to do the parenting (i.e., accept discipline and affection, follow rules, accept adult authority).

### Child/Professional Dyad

For the child in kinship care, the professional may have been the most stable and consistent adult throughout his or her life. The child's trust of, dependency on, and attachment to the worker may function as an obstacle to the child's transition into the caregiver's family.

Goals and issues for the child and professional include:

- identifying hierarchies, authority, and subordinate roles with respect to the caregiver (i.e., the caregiver as disciplinarian; the court as the determiner of placement);

- identifying how contact and communication will be maintained between the professional and child;

- giving the child "permission" to cooperate and attach to relatives without the professional feeling hurt, threatened, or abandoned;

- clarifying that family relationships are more important and lasting than friendships and professional relationships;

- preparing the child for the professional relationship eventually ending and being replaced by relationships with family and friends;

- minimizing the child's fantasies about the professional (i.e., friends for life, living with the professional);

- engaging in a loss and grief process related to changes in the relationship;

- clarifying a transfer of authority to the relative (i.e., "When your relative speaks, he speak for me also." "I expect you to listen to your relative the same way you listen to me.");

- identifying and minimizing the child's attempt to sabotage the separation (i.e., running away or acting out in order to keep the professional involved); and

- developing methods of conflict resolution and ways for the child to vent problems that do not result in the splitting or triangulating of the caregiver and parent.

## *Professional / Parent Dyad*
As the representative of authority and multiple agencies, the professional is a vulnerable target for the parent's anger, losses, projections, guilt, and fantasies. The quality of interaction between the professional and parent can affect the stability of the placement and the relative's ability to be a caregiver.

Clinical goals and issues for the professional and parent include:

- clarifying mutual roles, authority, expectations, and legal status in relation to the child, caregiver, and each other (professional and parent);

- identifying what the child and caregiver need from the parent in order to integrate as a family (i.e., parent's support and permission for the child to attach with the relative);

- addressing the parent's unresolved issues with previous professionals and agencies (to minimize the parent's projection, transference, competition, and sabotage);

- establishing a position of objectivity and fairness with the parent that is not biased by the child's or relative's feelings about the parent;

- engaging the parent in a loss and grief process related to the child and caregiver;

- engaging the parent in reality testing his or her fantasies; and

- establishing a dialogue on methods of problem solving and conflict resolution that will not split relationships or cause triangulation.

## Triads

Several triads exist that involve the child—the relative/child/parent triad, the relative/child/professional triad, and the parent/child/professional triad. Goals and clinical issues common to the three subsystems include:

- clarifying to the child the roles, relationships, responsibilities, and authority of the adults with respect to each other;

- clarifying the hierarchy of authority, responsibility, and decision making in relationship to the child;

- identifying to the child how decisions will be made and conflicts resolved in order to minimize splitting and triangulation;

- reviewing structural issues with the child (i.e., roles, methods of disciplining, rewards, schedules) so the child observes the adults in agreement and not vulnerable to splitting or manipulation;

- validating and reassuring each other's roles and authority by talking with the child in each other's presence;

- demonstrating to the child the adults' abilities to not be threatened by, compete with, or sabotage each other; and

- demonstrating to the child the adults' abilities to put aside unresolved issues from the past and work collaboratively in the best interest of the child.

Prior to involving the child, the caregiver, parent, and professional should meet to work on the issues above. In addition, this triad should develop techniques and strategies to present a unified coalition when with the child, and to avoid sabotaging the coalition.

The ultimate configuration for intervention is four dimensional. It includes the child, relative, parent, and professional. The triad goals (with and without the child) set forth above should be carried over in working with this configuration. This configuration may also be expanded to include the child's maternal and/or paternal extended family. Professionals should use the previously listed goals and clinical issues to structure the extended family's involvement in the intervention process.

## Motivational Approaches

Three approaches—a child focus, a family focus, and an individual focus—may be useful in motivating the family system to change and accept intervention. Many families are motivated by a combination of these approaches.

The *child-focus* approach is based on "the best interest of the child." The approach may be effective provided the family or parent defines and bases success on the success of the child, and places the child's needs before those of the adults.

The *family-focus* approach is based on "the best interests of the family." The approach may be useful when personal success is defined by the family's success, and the needs of the family take precedence over the needs of the individual.

An *individual focus* is based on "the best interest of the individual." This approach may be applicable to families whose philosophy is based on the beliefs that people must be able to help themselves before they can help others; that healthy independent individuals make healthy families; and that self-interest takes precedence to the child's or family's needs.

## Group Work Approaches with Kinship Families

Group work with kinship families may have multiple purposes: parent education and support, therapy, political advocacy, parent support, and child support. Groups may undertake one or several of these purposes.

## Caregiver Groups

Support groups for kinship caregivers may want to consider several topics:

- identifying and accessing financial systems (i.e., AFDC or TANF, Social Security, subsidized adoption, foster care funds);

- accessing medical and mental health care systems;

- accessing legal/judicial systems (i.e., family and civil court, child advocacy programs, legal aid services);

- accessing day care and educational services (i.e., Head Start, public/private day care, child study teams, special education resources and classes);

- managing the special medical and mental health care needs of children (i.e., HIV/AIDS, prenatal alcohol or drug exposure, physical/sexual abuse, hyperactivity);

- types and uses of medications and therapies;

- managing caregiver medical and health care issues (i.e., high blood pressure, diabetes, heart conditions, need for in-home services);

- respite, morbidity, and mortality planning;

- child rearing (approaches to limit setting and disciplining);

- information exchange (housing, employment, funding, community services);

- problem solving, brainstorming, venting, and emotional support;

- social activities, networking, and companionship;

- acquiring the legal rights/legal status of caregivers (i.e., adoption, foster parent, guardianship); and

- the emotional impact of relative placements on the child and parent.

## Therapeutic Groups

Therapeutic groups for kinship caregivers may also be useful in addressing issues of an emotional and psychodynamic nature, such as:

- engaging relatives in a loss and grief process (i.e., loss, anger, denial, guilt, mourning, acceptance);

- unresolved issues related to the parent (projection and transference to the child);

- attachment to and bonding with the child;

- eliciting, validating, and sharing the child's loss and grief;

- establishing boundaries and roles with the child and the parent;

- rejection by the child and split loyalties;

- managing competition with and sabotage by the parent;

- stress management;

- reestablishing a personal life and plans to obtain life cycle stages (i.e., retirement, leisure planning, a social life); and

- identifying and interrupting family legacies.

## Advocacy Groups

Political groups and organizations have developed in response to the need for and impact of federal, state, and local legislation on kinship families. Consequently, caregivers are becoming their own lobbyists and advocates, undertaking such activities as:

- reviewing existing legislation and drafting new policies and legislation affecting kinship families;

- developing community, state, and national organizations, networks, and parent groups;

- requiring participation and input on local and state agencies' advisory boards

- requiring participation on local, state, and federal task forces
- advocating for practices and policies by agencies that are sensitive and specific to kinship families.

## Parent Support and Therapeutic Groups

Support and therapeutic groups can be useful for parents whose children are in kinship care. Topics and issues may include:

- loss and separation;
- engaging in the loss and grief process;
- supporting the caregiver's role and authority;
- supporting the caregiver's and child's attachment;
- redefining roles and boundaries with the child and caregiver;
- legal rights of parents;
- avoiding triangulation of the child; and
- minimizing projection and transference.

## Child Support and Therapeutic Groups

Support and therapeutic groups for the child in kinship care may also be necessary. Many of the topics are similar to those suggested for the caregivers' and parents' groups, including:

- engaging in the loss and grief process;
- fantasies, loss, and separation;
- attachment to the kinship caregiver as a parental figure;
- split loyalty between the caregiver and the parent;
- abandonment/rejection by the parent;
- trauma, abuse, and neglect;
- redefining relationships and boundaries with the caregiver and parent; and

- understanding and managing special needs (i.e., medical, educational, or mental health).

## Additional Considerations

Logistical considerations for all of the groups include advertising, marketing, and timing of the groups; accessibility and transportation; location; day care; funding; and group empowerment and self-perpetuation.

Multiple family groups may also be necessary to address supportive and therapeutic issues. The participants in the groups may include the caregiver and child, the caregiver and parent, the parent and child, or the caregiver, parent, and child.

# Chapter Four
# *Case Management*

## Managing Clinical Services to the Family

### *Identifying Clinical Goals*

Following the assessment of clinical issues by family subsystem,* clinical goals and strategies should be organized and developed for each subsystem, using a systems and family approach. In addition, the professional should select an approach that will motivate family members to develop and achieve their goals.** The worker may select one or a combination of several approaches, depending on the goals and subsystem. Issues and goals will also need to be partialized and prioritized to lessen the family's feeling of being overwhelmed. A timetable for addressing clinical issues can help the family become focused and task oriented.

### *The Interface of Clients, Resources, and Services*

Once the approach and subsystem are set, appropriate services, agencies, and professionals should be identified. The selection of services and resources should be based on the family's clinical needs. Case managers should not underestimate the therapeutic value and impact of their position.

---

\* See the section of Chapter Three, "Assessment and Intervention," on *Intervention Strategies with Kinship Families.*
\*\* See the section of Chapter Three, "Assessment and Intervention," on *Motivational Approaches.*

A successful interface of clients with services and providers requires:

- the client's and service provider's mutual accessibility through the organization of transportation, appointment times, service location, child care, and work schedules; and

- the client's and provider's mutual understanding of and agreement on services, goals, and responsibility for achieving goals.

## Coordinating Case Management and Clinical Tasks

A communication system must be established between the case manager and the clinician. Once communication is established, the case manager and clinician can familiarize themselves with each other's plans; coordinate case management, clinical tasks, and goals in terms of priorities and timetables; identify the therapeutic impact of management tasks on clinical goals, and how the accomplishment of clinical goals may facilitate case management tasks; and establish a feedback system between themselves to evaluate the coordination of goals and tasks.

## Following Up and Evaluating the Family's Clinical Progress

Follow-up and evaluation tasks for the case manager include:

- acquiring progress reports from the clinician(s);

- reviewing and monitoring the client's use of services and the quality of those services;

- assessing the client's and provider's compatibility (i.e., goals, personalities, values, culture);

- assessing the extent to which goals, methods, and service plans are being accomplished;

- reformulating clinical issues, goals, and the selection of services and providers, if appropriate; and

- involving the client and the provider in mutual evaluations of each other's accomplishments of goals, tasks, and responsibilities.

# Managing Financial, Legal, Health Care, and Educational Tasks

## Managing Financial Tasks

Matching the family's financial needs to various financial resources and eligibility criteria is a major part of managing and developing a kinship family's financial plan. Tasks for the case manager include:

- determining what income the relative caregiver is already receiving on his or her own behalf (i.e., salary, unemployment, Social Security, retirement benefits);

- determining what income the caregiver is receiving for other adults and children in the household;

- determining who are the caregiver's legal dependents, who are informal dependents, and what is the status of any legal arrangements (i.e., foster care, adoption, guardianship, permanent/temporary custody);

- determining the biological relationships among all the children under the relative's care, the children and the kinship caregiver, and the kinship caregiver, the children, and other adults living in the household;

- determining what income is being received for the children and which adult is receiving that income;

- becoming familiar with all possible financial resource criteria (i.e., AFDC/TANF, Social Security, foster care, adoption subsidies)

- determining what the financial impact (i.e., losses or assets) would be if a caregiver selected certain sources of financial support;

- determining the feasibility of and tasks needed for meeting the eligibility criteria for specific funding sources (i.e., foster parent licensing, guardianship);

- providing technical assistance in securing documentation (i.e.,

Social Security cards, birth certificates, legal documents) necessary for completing financial applications; and

- advocating for, referring, and coordinating the family's needs and efforts with potential funding sources throughout the application, interview, and evaluation processes.

## *Managing Legal Tasks*

The case manager should work toward establishing a legal status for the child and caregiver that will maximize the family's stability and permanence. To accomplish this, the manager should:

- identify the biological relationship between the caregiver and the child in care, as well as the relationship between the caregiver and the child's parent;

- determine present, temporary, and long-term permanency plans for the children (i.e., permanent placement with relatives, eventual parent/child reunification);

- determine the feasibility of accomplishing the long-term permanency plan (i.e., effect of parent's history of addiction, relative's health, commitment of extended family);

- determine the compatibility between permanency planning and state/local timetables for implementing and reviewing permanency plans (i.e., the child's maximum length of stay in foster care);

- determine how extensive the caregiver's legal authority needs to be, based on the caregiver's, parent's, and extended family's relationships (i.e., hostile or compatible);

- compare the assets, limits, and compatibility of the caregiver's legal status with funding sources (i.e., adoption subsidy, foster parent subsidy);

- assist the family in securing legal services to petition for legal status; and

- refer family members to appropriate legal services if an adversarial situation should arrive (i.e., refer the caregiver and the parent to separate attorneys; refer the child to a guardian ad litem).

### *Managing Health Care Tasks*

Ensuring that kinship families have access to comprehensive services is a major challenge, due to the presence of multiple clients in many kinship families. In addition to any care needed by the child, elderly caregivers often have physical health problems, while the child's parent may need assistance with mental health problems. For example, a drug-addicted father may live in the home of his mother, who is caring for his child. The father's mental health problems will affect the kinship family's stability. Consequently, his mental health issues need to be addressed as part of a comprehensive service plan.

The case manager's tasks may include:

- determining each household members' individual physical and mental health status;

- determining which household members' health problems will be addressed in the family's service plan;

- identifying any prior history of services to the family's members;

- determining the family's history of appropriately accessing and using services;

- organizing and facilitating the family's access to and use of health care services;

- assisting family members in developing the skills and knowledge they need to independently advocate for and access health care services in their own behalf.

- accessing medical insurance sources (i.e., Medicare, Medicaid for children and elderly caregivers);

- being familiar with geriatric, pediatric, child, adolescent, and adult health and mental health services, given the wide age ranges of kinship family members;

- acquiring appropriate medical insurance to allow access to the family's preferred provider (i.e., HMOs may have their own provider and may chose not to cover the family's selection);

- coordinating the auxiliary and supportive services necessary for families to access health care services (i.e., day care, transportation); and

- updating and educating caregivers with respect to accepting therapy, understanding treatment, and administering medication to the children for physical and mental health problems.

### *Managing Educational Tasks*

The caseworker should work to increase the skills, understanding, and ability of the caregiver to meet the special educational needs of the child in care. Tasks include:

- determining the educational level, grade, and skills of the primary and secondary caregivers involved in the child's education (to ensure that the caregiver can help with homework or follow up with school or day care assignments/tasks for the child);

- determining the child's educational or special needs, what services have been provided, and what services are still needed;

- determining the family's and child's history of accessing and using educational services;

- determining or coordinating a developmental evaluation and the implementation of an individual educational plan for the child;

- educating the caregiver to the types of learning disabilities;

- referring and coordinating the caregiver's involvement with services that will educate and support him or her in managing the child's special needs (i.e., support groups for parents of children with attention deficient disorder);

- organizing the kinship and extended family to support the primary caregiver, if possible; and

- organizing and facilitating the necessary requests and services for accessing educational programs (i.e., transportation, school transfers, in-home services, after school programs, Head Start programs).

## Chapter Five
# *Race, Culture, and Other Special Considerations*

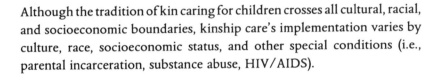

Although the tradition of kin caring for children crosses all cultural, racial, and socioeconomic boundaries, kinship care's implementation varies by culture, race, socioeconomic status, and other special conditions (i.e., parental incarceration, substance abuse, HIV/AIDS).

## Racial and Cultural Considerations

A series of questions must be considered when intervening in or deciding to use kinship families as a placement resource.

- What are the roles, hierarchy, and authority of relatives in the raising of children, in both the presence or absence of parents?

- What is the family's hierarchy of responsible relatives (i.e., godparents, grandparents, siblings) in the temporary or permanent absence of parents?

- Does the family practice or reject formal or informal placement of relative's children (i.e., adoption, guardianship)?

- How do gender and cultural traditions affect the family's decision-making structure, child-rearing practices, and selection of a family spokesperson?

- What has been/is the family's experience and attitude towards social service professionals and institutions?

- What has been/is the legal or social service agency's reputation in a given community or culture?

- What are the family's and culture's child-rearing practices and attitudes?

- How have environmental conditions or changes affected the family's socioeconomic stability, child-rearing practices, and family members (i.e., unemployment, migration, housing, rural or urban settings, language)?

- What are the family's attitudes about the use of foster care or kinship care, the termination of a parent's rights, or parental contact with children after termination of parental rights?

- Have staff been trained and sensitized to the culture of the families being served?

- Have community members or consumers of services been involved in legitimizing and informing the community and its families of the services being offered?

- Do the program's staffing patterns adequately represent the cultures and races being served?

- Have structural mechanisms been developed to guarantee the community's input and evaluation of services being given (i.e., establishment of an advisory committee, service evaluations by consumers)?

## Incarceration and Substance Abuse

The family dynamics associated with substance abuse and parental incarceration also impact the provision of kinship care. These clinical issues and dynamics include legacies, codependency, recidivism, anger, embarrassment, guilt, and loyalty.

Children whose parents are substance abusers or incarcerated are predisposed to repeat family patterns of addiction and recidivism (legacies) due to the existence of and exposure to reinforcements in the family (i.e., role models, value systems, environmental factors, and attachments) and to the child's need to be accepted by and identify with his or her family and parent.

Codependency is also associated with addictive and recidivistic behaviors. Codependent family members often

- enable or allow a dependent person to do something that hurts him/herself or the codependent person;

- are totally concerned with others, and neglect themselves or other responsibilities;

- take or accept responsibility for another's life or problems, and don't allow others to be responsible for themselves;

- are unable to allow others to become independent, due to a perceived loss of purpose or out of fear of the other person's failure or success;

- are unable to distinguish their own feelings and thoughts from those of others; and

- define their self-worth, direction, or purpose on the basis of other's approval, goals, problems, or expectations.

The anger, embarrassment, and guilt that accompany the placement of a child into kinship care are intensified if the parent is involved in illegal activities. The stigma of the parent being "different" now escalates to one of the parent being a "criminal."

In addition to the loyalty issues discussed earlier in this volume, families in which the kinship placement is due to parental substance abuse or incarceration must confront the following scenarios:

- The caregiver or child may assume codependency roles that they believe demonstrate loyalty (i.e., enabling, joining, exonerating, denying, or justifying the parent's or family's problems).

- The child may repeat the legacy as a way of showing loyalty to or establishing a common bond with the parent or family.

- The child or relative may display anger with family members who do not assume (codependency) roles in support of the parent (i.e., who do not allow the parent to live in the home while involved in addictive or criminal activities).

As with loyalty issues, the intervention goals and approaches with kinship families discussed earlier still apply, with the following additions. The worker should

- minimize the child, parent, relative, and family's codependent roles and behavior (i.e., denial, enabling, joining);

- refer the parent to appropriate services to address addiction or recidivism;

- use individual, dyad, and triad interventions to assist family members in identifying and appropriately directing anger and embarrassment with the parent (a process that may also need to occur with the kinship caregiver if he or she was the predecessor of the family's legacies);

- enable the kinship caregiver to eliminate or minimize the child's exposure to family members, households, or role models who perpetuate the family's legacies (i.e., not allow criminal activities to occur, prevent addicted individuals from residing in the home);

- help the parent and caregiver to discourage the child from and free the child of any obligation to repeat the family's legacies;

- have the parent and caregiver redefine to the child common goals and values for bonding, attachment, and new family legacies (i.e., sobriety, education, noncriminal behavior, nonviolence); and

- establish support systems within the household and environment to reinforce the family's new legacies (i.e., therapy, housing, employment, job readiness, education).

The parent may be absent from or inaccessible to the child due to permanent or temporary incarceration or residential substance abuse treatment. Additional interventions may be required to address these issues and the reunification of the parent with the child, such as

- engaging the family (i.e., parent, child, and caregiver) in a process to handle the loss, guilt, anger, denial, and grief related to the parent's absence;

- redefining the caregiver's and parent's role and authority in child rearing, decision making, and nurturing during the parent's absence;

- assisting the caregiver and parent in explaining and demonstrating the change in roles and authority to the child;

- establishing lines of communication (i.e., phone, visits, letters) among the parent, caregiver, and child;

- establishing processes for conflict resolution, input, and decision making; and

- helping the child develop a repertoire of explanations and skills to explain and cope with comments about the parent's absence (i.e., "I heard your parent is a lifer for homicide").

If the permanency plan calls for reunification of the child with his or her parent, then the worker must

- prepare the parent for the child's testing and rejection of the parent's role, authority, or nurturance;

- prepare the parent for testing and disbelief from the child, relative, or family of the parent's rehabilitation;

- develop a transitional process between the parent and relative for the gradual sharing and exchanging of parental roles;

- engage the child in a loss and grief process related to the loss of the parental relationship with the relative caregiver (i.e., accepting the change, redefining the relationship, maintaining contact and communication); and

- develop a repertoire for explaining or coping with comments about the parent's return, the relative's absence, or the role change.

# HIV/AIDS

When a parent dies from AIDS, the kinship family is strongly affected by the pre- and postmortem bereavement associated with a terminal illness, as well as the social stigma attached to HIV infection. Although the loss and grief process is not unique to kinship families, these families may need additional assistance as they experience the dual loss associated with kinship care and the loss of a primary member to AIDS. The family's journey through the typical stages of grief may be interrupted, prolonged, or even have begun prior to the parent's death, and may be characterized by a variety of experiences and emotions that are not usually part of the grieving process.

Although shock is associated with almost all deaths, the families of those affected by AIDS also experience shock resulting from the degenerative and prolonged nature of the disease. Such shock is frequently associated with sudden, prolonged, and terminal illnesses such as cancer, and can occur despite the family's preparation.

The family grieving the death of a parent from AIDS may also experience embarrassment as it works its way through the grieving process, resulting from the implicit assumptions about the deceased's lifestyle and morals (i.e., drug use, sexual activities), the assumed negative reflections on the family, or the public awareness of and stigma associated with the cause of death. Anger may also arise from the caregiver's or child's:

- feelings that the deceased was indulgent, irresponsible, and inconsiderate of the consequences of his or her behavior and the impact of those behaviors on the family;

- misconceptions about contagion and the associated fear of having been infected from contact with the deceased;

- embarrassment due to the cause of death; or

- perceived need for secretiveness with the deceased's children, family, and friends about the parent's death or cause of death;

Guilt often results from a lack of awareness of the illness and not having had more time to respond or be supportive. The child and caregiver may also experience guilt for:

- withdrawing support or feeling revulsion and fear of the individual with AIDS;

- feeling relief when the parent died;

- feeling embarrassed and angry toward the deceased; or

- unresolved issues from the past with the deceased about AIDS or other subjects.

The mourning process is often characterized or interrupted by recollections of embarrassment, anger, and guilt that may overshadow and outweigh positive memories. The parent or child may avoid the mourning process in an attempt to avoid painful memories and feelings of guilt, anger, or embarrassment, or because of feelings that the deceased is undeserving of mourning.

Children or caregivers who enters the denial stage of the grieving process may be characterized by not admitting to feelings of anger, embarrassment, shock, guilt, or the need for mourning. They may deny the cause of illness before and/or after the parent's death.

Acceptance of the parent's death can also be interrupted by the nondisclosure of the parent's cause of death to relatives and friends. The child or caregiver may be unable to acknowledge being a relative of the deceased or be unable to negotiate the stages of the bereavement process.

## Chapter Six
# *Legal Relationships*

Marie is 22 years old and has two children, ages three and five. Marie had been working to earn her GED when she got involved with what her mother describes as "the wrong crowd." Marie's 43-year-old mother, Patricia, watched as her daughter's life slowly deteriorated.

Despite the fact that Marie rarely attended her GED classes, she relied on her mother more and more often to baby-sit the children. Sometimes she would leave them overnight without warning. Overnights increased to weekends before Patricia confronted her daughter about what she suspected was a drug addiction. Marie agreed to enter a 90-day inpatient drug treatment program and Patricia agreed to assume parenting responsibilities in her absence. Both Marie and Patricia were hopeful that Marie would bounce back after a successful three-month recovery to resume full-time care of her children.

Patricia is now a kinship caregiver, a relative providing full-time parenting to her young grandchildren. For generations, extended families have made arrangements to provide care for children whose parents are unable to do so. These caregiving relationships differ according to the parents' and the families' needs. For example, children whose mothers have recently died from AIDS may require permanent, full-time care from a family member; a mother who must fulfill a short-term military assignment, on the other hand, may require less assistance. Grandmothers may offer a rural reprieve to their inner-city grandchildren during their summer vacation or may step in as full-time parents following a mother's fatal accident.

Legislatures have only recently begun to recognize the dramatic increase in these relative caregiving relationships. Few laws speak directly to the situations that these grandparents, aunts, and uncles face. Thus, kinship caregivers have sought and achieved varying levels of legal approval for their "unplanned parenthood," conforming themselves to the legal status that seems most appropriate to their experience. Many caregivers never involve the courts in their family's situation and never see the need to formalize their caregiving relationship. Others encounter welfare workers, doctors, and school administrators who demand proof of legal custody. Still others adopt their kin, trading in their status as "grandma" or "aunt" to become the child's legal parent.

This chapter discusses the various legal options that are available to relatives embarking on a caregiving relationship, outlines the rights of the caregiver and the parent under each arrangement, and suggests some of the advantages and limits of each legal relationship.

## Informal Caregiving

The overwhelming majority of kinship caregivers never see the inside of a courtroom or seek the approval of a judge. In these situations, the caregiver has physical custody only. Physical custody is the actual physical care and supervision of a child, and might include day-to-day parenting responsibilities such as feeding and clothing a child. In most of these cases, the parent agrees to have a relative care for the child, either through an explicit arrangement or through abandonment. In the above case study, for example, Patricia agreed to assume physical custody of the children while Marie sought drug treatment.

Even if Patricia takes no further legal action, some rights do attach to her informal caregiving status. Most importantly, informal caregivers can apply for and receive public assistance for the children. Funds from programs such as Temporary Assistance for Needy Families (TANF), the recent successor to the Aid to Families with Dependent Children (AFDC) program, are available to relative caregivers; nonrelatives who are parenting may receive general assistance. When determining a relative caregiver's eligibility for public assistance, it is the child's income, not the caregiver's, that should be considered. Grandparents and other relatives have no legal responsibility to provide for their young kin and their income cannot be automatically attributed to the child's care. Thus, even if Patricia has a steady job with an income level that would disqualify her for public assistance, she may still be able to receive TANF for her grandchildren because neither Marie nor the children's father is contributing to their care. Kinship caregivers who are themselves eligible for TANF should take care to note that if the child is added to the caregiver's grant, benefits may be limited to 60 months for the entire group, including the child.

To be eligible for benefits, the relative caregiver must prove that he or she is the child's primary physical custodian. This requirement does not translate into a requirement that the caregiver obtain legal custody. Unfortunately, both caregivers and caseworkers frequently misunderstand this distinction and eligible and deserving caregivers often experience delays in receiving necessary financial assistance. In lieu of legal custody papers, a caregiver may prove that he or she has assumed primary parenting responsibilities by bringing the child to the intake appointment or by providing relevant documentation such as a letter from a parent, a child and youth worker, or another authority figure. It is illegal for a caseworker to make legal custody a prerequisite for the receipt of public assistance; any caregiver who is turned away for this reason should ask to speak with a supervisor.

Benefits to a short-term caregiver like Patricia may be delayed while the local welfare agency closes the parent's case and transfers the child to the caregiver's newly opened case. By the time this process is completed, the parent may be ready to regain physical custody of the child. Fortunately, in many jurisdictions an expedited procedure has been developed for cases in which the parent is a substance abuser. If a grandparent or other kinship caregiver alleges that a child's parent is a drug user, the caseworker can open the caregiver's case immediately.

Thus, the parent and the caregiver will both receive grants for a period of time until the caseworker is able to verify the parent's information and terminate the parent's assistance.

Along with the right to receive public assistance for the children in their care, physical custodians like Patricia also assume the responsibility for making everyday parenting decisions regarding the children's care. For example, physical custodians may set bedtimes, establish disciplinary rules, and provide for the child's basic need for food, clothing, and shelter.

Since many changes in responsibility are accomplished informally, the transfer of physical custody can represent more of a practical than a legal change. Common sense dictates that the adult caring for the child would provide for the child's daily needs, but a change in caregivers does not itself trigger a change in legal status. Under the law, the parent is still responsible for the child, retaining the right to control all religious and educational decisions. In fact, many schools may refuse to allow a caregiver to enroll a child in school without proof of a change in legal custody. Other schools adhere to requirements similar to the public assistance standard described above, demanding proof only that the child resides full-time with the relative. Without a transfer of legal custody, however, it is the parent who is entitled to receive school records and to attend any educational planning meetings regarding the child.

The most problematic obstacle faced by physical custodians, however, is the lack of authority to consent to the child's medical care. Many informal caregivers find creative ways to maneuver around the requirement that a parent consent to medical treatment. For example, the doctor at the local clinic may know Patricia and Marie's family well. The doctor may have treated Marie when she was younger or Patricia may have accompanied Marie and the grandchildren to several past appointments. Doctors who are familiar with a family's situation may accept the caregiver as the parental authority, even without legal custody. Other doctors may recognize the prevalence of nontraditional families in their area and scrutinize their patients' caregivers less closely. A caregiver might also search to locate a parent every time a child requires medical treatment. Many caregivers, however, are forced to rely on hospital emergency rooms to provide all of the child's medical care. With few or no available alternatives, the caregiver waits until an urgent situation arises and then requests a full medical examination, in addition to the emergency care, for the child.

Two jurisdictions have passed legislation designed to remove this obstacle to medical treatment. California and the District of Columbia both enacted medical consent laws in 1994 that enable a caregiver to make general medical decisions without petitioning for full custodial rights. In California, the legislation directs the relative to sign a notarized affidavit, stating that he or she is the child's full-time caregiver. The affidavit then entitles the relative caregiver to enroll the child in school and to authorize general medical and dental care. For nonrelative caregivers, the affidavit allows the caregiver to enroll the child in school, but to consent only to school-related medical care (i.e., immunizations and physicals). By requiring only the caregiver's signature, such mechanisms are especially effective in situations where the parent cannot be located.

Under the District of Columbia approach, a parent must sign a medical consent affidavit, but the form need not be notarized. The caregiver's authorization is limited to medical consent only and does not authorize the caregiver to enroll the child in school. The law does not provide for children whose parents have disappeared and cannot be located. As legislatures around the country become more aware of the difficulties facing relative caregivers, the legislation and experiences of the District of Columbia and California will provide useful models.

Without easy access to medical care and school enrollment, the informal caregiving relationship is less than optimal, both for the caregiver who is struggling to provide for the child's needs and for the child who is seeking stability and predictability. Additionally, children in informal care may be bounced from parent to grandparent and back again, depending on the parent's whim. Only a court's custody order can protect children from this uncertainty and potential risk. Regardless of how "unfit" the parent is, the parent still retains full custodial rights and may "snatch" the child from the caregiver's home at any time. Thus, even if

Marie fails to complete her drug treatment program and/or experiences a relapse, she still retains the legal right to take her children from Patricia's home. Of course, Patricia or any other interested person may attempt to report Marie for child abuse or neglect if they believe that she is unable to care for her children and is putting them at risk. Such allegations, however, are often hotly contested, difficult to prove, and emotionally hard on the adults and children alike.

On the other hand, informal caregiving relationships avoid the family strife that often results from court involvement. While Marie may agree that her children should be living with their grandmother, she may view the filing of a custody petition as a hostile action, especially if Patricia is required to detail her daughter's drug history. Many parents also misunderstand the scope and duration of custody, confusing it with adoption. They fear that a transfer of legal custody will strip them of all rights to see their children or to be involved with their lives. What was an amicable and agreeable situation before a custody petition was filed can unfortunately dissolve into a cross fire of accusations before the judge.

Mediation or other forms of alternative dispute resolution might help a family to come to an agreement about the care and custody of a child. Many jurisdictions are requiring that family members participate in court-sponsored mediation programs before they bring a custody case to court for a contest and a ruling. The trained mediator attempts to give everyone an equal voice in the process and to help sort out emotional issues that might cloud the best interests of the child. Power dynamics are important in these situations, as family members can sometimes exert undue influence over each other; indeed, mediation should not be used when there are clear disparities in the personal power between the members. A family therapist might also play this mediating role, so long as the individuals clarify who the client is and what the bounds of confidentiality are in the group.

Informal caregiving relationships have another benefit, this one arising from necessity. An informal arrangement is often the only way to deal with an immediate crisis or a short-term situation such as a brief period of incarceration. In many jurisdictions, the process for acquiring legal custody is long and drawn-out. In Philadelphia, for example, a grandmother who petitions for custody may wait nine months before seeing a judge and obtaining a custody order. Thus, most kinship caregivers go through a period of informal caregiving even when their eventual goal is to acquire legal custody.

# Legal Custody

When Marie first enters her drug rehabilitation program, she has every intention of returning to parent her children. She and her mother agree to a transfer of physical custody and make interim arrangements with doctors and teachers for Patricia to care for the children's needs. After two weeks at her program, however, Marie is unable to stay clean. She disappears from the treatment center and Patricia does not hear from her for over a week. Finally, Patricia hears word from a neighborhood friend that Marie is hanging out with her old crowd and is back to using drugs. Patricia is disappointed, but continues to believe that Marie will eventually get her life on track and resume care of her children. In the short month that she has had the children, Patricia is struggling to adjust her life to her new responsibilities. She has lost touch with many of her own friends and she recently withdrew from her church's choir—"temporarily," she tells them, promising she will be back in time to rehearse for the Christmas concert.

Recognizing that her caregiving responsibilities may continue longer than anticipated and struggling to provide financially for the children, Patricia applies for AFDC. Marie drops in occasionally for visits. Usually she just plays with the children for an hour or two in Patricia's home, but sometimes she takes them out. Patricia does not know where Marie is living and she has heard that Marie spends most of her time using drugs, but she knows (because Marie reminds her) that without custody, she cannot deny Marie the chance to visit with and even take the children. Besides, her grandchildren are always so happy to see their mother.

Then, one weekend, Marie does not return with the children on Sunday night as promised. For two agonizing days, Patricia waits by the phone while neighbors and friends try to locate Marie. When the children finally return on Wednesday, they eagerly rush into their grandmother's arms. Marie is offended by Patricia's questions and the suggestion that the children were at any risk. She becomes hostile, reminding Patricia that, "I am their mother and I'll take them whenever I want for as long as I want." Patricia's instincts tell her that Marie would not intentionally harm the children and she feels sure that she would tire of caring for them after more than a few days. Regardless, she does not like the instability that she feels and she fears for the children's safety. It is at this point that she decides to apply for legal custody.

When a child is born, both biological parents—married or unmarried—have legal custody. *Legal custody* is the right to make major decisions affecting the best interest of a minor child, including medical, religious, and educational decisions. For parents who are living together and sharing parenting responsibilities, legal custody is rarely a source of contention. The parents share time with their child and cooperate with decision making, and each parent is responsible for ensuring that the child is fed, clothed, and provided for.

Grandparents and other kinship care providers can only become legal caregivers for a child by petitioning the court. A transfer of legal custody only occurs when a judge signs a formal custody order. Even if a grandmother or godparent raises a child from birth, with no assistance or input from either parent, legal custody still remains with that child's parents. A parent who writes and signs a letter turning her child over to a relative may have assisted the caregiver in acquiring benefits or accessing medical care, but she has not transferred legal custody. Thus, despite the fact that Marie will be in treatment away from her children, unable to make contact with or provide for them, she still remains their legal custodian (as does their father, assuming that a custody order has not been entered against him).

Custody procedures differ from state to state. Some states talk in terms of "guardianship" rather than "custody." Although the terminology may differ, custody and guardianship share similar characteristics. In both cases, some—but not all—parenting responsibilities are transferred from the parent to the legal custodian or guardian. As legal custodian, the caregiver has the right to make basic medical decisions, to enroll the child in school, to sign school forms such as report cards, to make decisions involving special education services (including the child's Individual Education Program or IEP), and to take the child to the religious services of the caregiver's choice. In addition, just as the physical custodian takes on the practical responsibility for providing food, clothing, and shelter, the legal custodian not only provides these things for the child, but is legally obligated to do so. Now, if the child is neglected, it is the legal custodian rather than the parent who will be held liable.

## *Standing*

Although custody procedures may vary from state to state, the person desiring custody must always have "standing" to petition the court. The doctrine of standing requires that a person be sufficiently connected to a child, or be so affected by the court's potential decision, as to have earned the court's recognition in a dispute involving that child's life. With standing, a person gets to initiate court action, seek a remedy, and even frame the legal issues; without standing, the person may find it difficult to access the court process at all.

The standing requirement prevents outsiders from interfering in a family's or a child's life. For example, Patricia's neighbor may be acutely aware of Marie's drug problem and of her inability to care for her children. She may be willing to care for the children herself. Despite her genuine concern, however, she does not have standing and a court would not entertain her custody petition.

Parents automatically have standing in custody cases involving their children. Grandparents and other relative caregivers, however, must prove that they have an "in loco parentis" relationship with the child they are caring for. An adult who stands in loco parentis to a child stands in the place of the parent and has actually assumed the parents' caregiving duties and responsibilities. A person standing in loco parentis buys food and clothing for the child, ensures that the child attends school, and meets the child's emotional and physical needs. A person need not be a relative to achieve this status, but he or she must be the child's physical custodian and must have been providing care for a significant period of time. Thus, a family friend who has raised a nonrelative child from birth to age two may have standing to file a custody petition, while a grandmother who worries about the inadequate care that her grandchildren are receiving, but is not caring for them, will not.

This is not to say that the concerned grandmother may not intervene on behalf of her grandchildren. As noted earlier, anyone who observes a child being neglected or abused may make a report to their local children's services agency and may eventually be considered as a potential caregiver. Thus, if her grandchildren are being neglected by their parents, a grandmother may allege that the children are "dependent"—without proper parental care and control—and may request that the children's services agency and the courts intervene on their behalf. One possible result of this intervention would be placement of the children with the grandmother and court-awarded custody.

Once Patricia has had her grandchildren for a few months, she is likely to meet the standing requirements. Marie is not contributing to the children's care in any way. She does not parent them and she makes no financial contributions to their food or clothing. Although Marie does visit the children occasionally and does continue to maintain her relationship with them, this does not undermine the fact that Patricia is the children's primary caregiver.

## The Court Process

Once the standing requirement is met and the custody petition is filed, a hearing will be held in which the court will determine what is best for each child. While the law favors biological parents over all other relatives and nonrelatives, the standard that the judge applies in making a custody determination is the "best interest of the child." The judge will look for the adult who is best able to provide a stable home for the child. The judge will inquire as to who provides food and clothing for the child, who ensures that the child does homework, and who provides discipline and structure in the child's life. Factors such as a parent's drug problem or nomadic housing pattern will weigh against the parent.

If the judge decides that the relative caregiver is the adult best situated to care for the child, a custody order will be signed by the judge. Custody orders occupy an interesting time frame in that they have the potential to be both temporary and permanent. If no one ever attempts to modify the order by returning to court—for example, if Marie never completes her drug rehab and never expresses an interest in regaining custody of her children—then the order will continue until each of the children reaches age 18. There is no time limit to Patricia's legal custody. On the other hand, if the parent achieves a "significant change" in her life situation—if Marie kicks her drug habit and secures adequate housing—then she will have an opportunity to file a petition, seeking modification of the custody order. A custody order does not terminate the parent's rights, and, with the court's approval, legal custody can always be transferred back to the parent.

The adversarial nature of custody proceedings can be destructive to the family unit. Patricia will have to tell the judge that Marie is a drug addict. She will have to outline for strangers her own daughter's shortcomings as a parent. In order to reduce this conflict, most courts provide an opportunity for the parties to either enter into a pretrial agreement or to resolve their differences through mediation. If Marie agrees that her children are better off with their grandmother, then she and Patricia may enter into an agreement that states merely that Marie is not currently able to care for her children. Similarly, mediation programs allow the parties to have an "off-the-record" discussion, often with specially trained lawyers or mental health professionals, to determine cooperatively what custody arrangement would be most beneficial to the children. If the parties are not able to agree, a hearing is scheduled with a judge, but if they can agree, the family is spared the pain of a public airing of family grievances. In either case, the parties should obtain a written court order for their later use.

As part of the custody process, visiting issues are also decided.

Grandparents and other kinship caregivers should enter the hearing with a specific idea of the visiting schedule that they would like to see implemented. How often would the children like to see their parents? How often is it reasonable to expect the parent to be able to attend visits? Great care must be taken in formulating a visiting plan so that the children will have adequate time with their parents without setting such high expectations that the parent is likely to fail. For example, Marie may initially state that she would like to see her children every other weekday with a longer visit every weekend, but she must also remember that she has issues of her own to take care of and that any missed visit will be disappointing to her children. On the other hand, given Marie's past behavior, Patricia will have concerns about allowing Marie to take the children on unsupervised visits. She may press the judge to restrict the visits to her home or, if the judge feels strongly that Marie should have unsupervised time with the children, to ask for a visiting schedule that is clearly specified.

Having legal custody provides the kinship caregiver with many tangible benefits. The custody order enables the caregiver to enroll the children in school, access medical care, and apply for benefits, all with little or no hassle. The custody process also provides a forum for the caregiver and the parents to work out important visiting details and gives the caregiver an enforceable legal document to fall back on should the parent violate the court's order.

One note about lawyers and the custody process: though parties to court custody actions are allowed to be represented by a lawyer of their choosing, few courts appoint or pay for lawyers for parents and adult caregivers. In many locales, as many as three-quarters (or more) of all custody litigants cannot afford counsel and so proceed *pro se*—on their own or "for one's self." Many of the technical legal issues and rules of custody law can be overlooked in *pro se* cases. To ease this burden, some communities have developed self-help guides or even clinics to advise and train lay people who must represent themselves. For example, in Philadelphia, KIDS CAP (Custody Assistance Project) is staffed by volunteer lawyers and law students who give free advice to *pro se* litigants. Lawyers or other persons serving as guardians ad litem are sometimes appointed by the court to represent a child's interests, but this, too, is rare and may not necessarily help in all situations. The question always remains: What will help the court determine what is best for the child?

The intangible benefits of legal custody are impressive, especially for the children involved. Legal custody can mark the beginning of a period of stability that the children have not known before. The children no longer need to worry about where they will be living next week or next month. They can settle into school and trust that their teachers and neighborhood friends will remain constant. In situations where a visiting plan has been worked out, the children can eagerly anticipate seeing their parents at regularly scheduled times. Most importantly for the child who has lived with an inconsistent, indifferent, or neglectful parent, the kinship caregiver is the first person to step forward and say, "I want this child. I choose to be responsible for her." To many children, this psychological stability is the greatest gift of all.

## Formal Kinship Foster Care

Informal caregiving relationships and legal custody transfers usually occur with little or no involvement by the local children's services agency. Often a relative sees that the parent's situation is declining and steps in before the child is in real danger of neglect or abuse. Or the parent may recognize that he is unable to care for his children and may approach a relative or friend about assuming parenting responsibilities. In other cases, the local children's services agency is only briefly involved, stating to a mother, for example, that her child will be removed if she does not voluntarily place the child with a responsible relative.

For kinship caregivers who either desire continued children's services involvement or do not object to it, however, formal kinship foster care may be a viable option. For many years, relatives were denied the opportunity to become paid caregivers for their kin. If they wanted to care for their grandchildren, nieces, and nephews, the relatives were told that they must accept legal custody and rely on AFDC and community programs for support. They were denied access to foster care payments and to the many services available to foster parents (i.e., therapy, day care, respite care). In addition, each caregiver became his or her own case manager, locating and coordinating all of the many services and agencies that the children required.

The AFDC rates available to relative caregivers were dramatically lower than the foster care rates paid to nonrelative foster parents. For example, in California in 1989, a grandmother caring for her grandchild would receive an average of $326 per month for one child, while a nonrelative foster parent would receive $450.* Compounding this disparity was the basing of the AFDC system on a belief in economies of scale. Specifically, a grandmother who received $250 per month for one grandchild would not see her AFDC check double if she began caring for a second grandchild. Instead, she received a decreased amount for the second child. The more children a grandmother agreed to care for, the less money she received per child. In contrast, foster care rates remain constant. A foster parent who cares for three children receives roughly three times the amount that a foster parent with one child receives.

A decision in 1995 by the U.S. Supreme Court, *Anderson v. Edwards*, may further this inequity. Federal AFDC rules required states to group each member of a household's nuclear family into a single AFDC "assistance unit." In reviewing California's "nonsibling filing unit rule," the Supreme Court decided that when states are calculating the amount of an AFDC grant, they can count into a single "assistance unit" all needy children who live in the same household, whether or not they are siblings. Previously, kinship caregivers could receive separate grants for different sibling groups in their household. Under the California rule, however, consolidation of assistance units results in a lower financial payment to the caregiver. Other states, including Pennsylvania, have traditionally counted a kinship-placed child as a "household of one" so as not to financially penalize the caregiver. Each state will likely characterize grant-group members differently under the new TANF program.

---

* Minkler, M., & Roe, K. M. (1993). *Grandmothers as caregivers: Raising children of the crack cocaine epidemic*. Newbury Park, CA: Sage, p. 93.

Given the increased services and financial support available to foster parents, many kin are attracted to the foster care option. In 1979, the U.S. Supreme Court ruled in *Miller v. Youakim* that relatives could not be arbitrarily excluded from participating in foster care programs. Relative caregivers can still be required to meet all standard foster care requirements (i.e., adequate number of bedrooms, criminal and child abuse clearances, training) and states are not required to help relatives meet these requirements, but states cannot not exclude otherwise eligible relatives merely because of their familial relationship to the child.

Since the U.S. Supreme Court's decision in *Miller v. Youakim*, some children's services agencies have developed specific kinship foster care programs, while others continue to resist the idea of paying foster care rates to relatives caring for their own kin. Critics argue that family members should not demand payment for filling a role that is already morally theirs. Others question whether a parent whose adult child is drug addicted can really parent a new generation of children. Critics worry that the caregiver will not fully understand the importance of the foster care regulations and procedures and may allow the parent to have unauthorized contact with the child, putting the child at risk. Still others have pointed to the financial disincentives to reunification that arise when relatives become kinship foster care providers, since a child's parents would not be entitled to the higher foster care rates (i.e., a group of three children placed in foster care with their grandmother would experience a significant drop in income on their return to their parent's home).

To become a kinship foster care provider, the relative caregiver must allow the children's services agency to take custody of the child. Grandparents and other relatives are often hesitant to do so out of fear that the child will be placed in another foster home or will be too easily removed from their home should they misstep in even the slightest way. Similarly, kinship caregivers wonder if, in licensing their homes for formal foster care, they are opening themselves to the possibility of having other nonrelative children placed with them. Most states have managed to work through these concerns, but, without legal custody, the caregiver experiences a loss of control that makes some relatives wary.

Once Patricia and Marie have worked out their informal caregiving relationship and negotiated a transfer of custody, Patricia will have a difficult time achieving formal foster parent status. Legally, Patricia could surrender custody of her grandchildren to her local children's services agency with an agreement that they would re-place the children in her home as kinship foster children. Because of the added cost to the state, however, many agencies are reluctant to perform this transfer.

Imagine instead that Marie asks a neighbor to sit with her children while she "runs to the store." Instead, Marie disappears on one of her binges. After two days with no word from Marie, the neighbor is no longer able to care for the children and contacts the local police or child abuse hot line to report the abandoned children. The children are placed in emergency foster care while children's services investigates the situation. As soon as Patricia is notified of her grandchildren's predicament, she calls the social worker and notifies him that she is interested in caring for the children. They discuss the kinship foster care option and Patricia's house is investigated and approved by a local foster care agency.

As a kinship foster parent, Patricia has surprisingly few rights. In return for the foster care payment that she will receive, Patricia has agreed that her grandchildren will remain in the custody of the state. Foster parents are very involved in their children's lives, making everyday decisions about bedtimes, meals, and discipline. Because they do not have legal custody, however, they are not authorized to consent to medical care or to sign off on important school decisions. A kinship foster parent who presents herself as "Grandma" or "Aunt Harriet" might gain access to more information and decision making than would a traditional foster parent, but technically, the legal rights reserved to kinship foster care providers are few.

The rights not transferred to Patricia as a foster parent will remain with Marie for as long as her parental rights remain intact. Marie will retain the right to be involved in educational decisions (i.e., IEPs) and will be contacted to consent for all nonroutine medical care. Most foster care agencies have authorization forms that a parent can sign transferring minimal authority to the agency (and therefore the foster parent), but none of these parental rights are automatically transferred to the grandparent.

The obvious benefit of kinship foster care over legal custody is the extensive network of support available to both the kinship caregiver and the parent. In addition to higher monthly payments, Patricia will receive the support of her foster care social worker, who can help her to manage the children's medical and mental health appointments and to coordinate (and pay for) other services that the family might need, such as day care or respite care. Similarly, the worker will be an ally to Patricia in her struggle to help Marie. If the long-term goal for the children is reunification with their mother, then the state is required under federal law to make "reasonable efforts" to achieve that goal. The worker will help locate and make referrals to drug treatment programs for Marie and, as appropriate, will help to facilitate regular family visits. This might involve providing car fare to the parent or supervising visits where concerns exist about the parent's ability to interact safely with the child.

For cases involving severe neglect, abuse, or other painful family dynamics, continued involvement by the children's services agency may be not only appealing but essential. Guided by clear foster care regulations and supervised closely by agency social workers, relative caregivers may be better equipped to protect children who are still at risk. For those families in which the relative caregiver is unable to set limits with a drug-addicted or inconsistent parent, safeguards can be established with agency workers, child advocates, and therapists to protect the child.

For other families, however, kinship foster care presents too much of a burden. Competent and independent caregivers who do not require the assistance of agency social workers may resent the increased scrutiny inherent in being a licensed foster care provider. After raising four of her own children, Patricia may be insulted by a requirement that she attend foster parent training, especially if it does not address her unique status as an older second-time parent. Patricia may choose to forfeit foster care's additional money and services for the sake of increasing her independence and control.

# Adoption

The most permanent and stable legal relationship that can be forged between relative caregivers and the children in their care is the kinship adoption. No special concessions are made to a grandparent, aunt, or uncle who is adopting a biologically related child, and both parents' rights must be legally terminated. Unlike a transfer of custody, the termination of a parent's rights is irrevocable. The parent cannot merely petition the court for a change when the circumstances of his or her life improve.

To adopt a child, the relative caregiver will have to involve the courts and will very likely need to hire an attorney. Parental rights can be terminated voluntarily (when parentz agree to sign voluntary relinquishment papers) or involuntarily (by proving at a hearing that the parents have, through actions or omissions, surrendered their right to parent the child). Once the court signs an order terminating the parents' rights, a second hearing is held to approve and legalize the adoption.

Once the adoption is legalized by the court, the adopting relative assumes all of the rights and responsibilities formerly held by the parents and the parents' legal connection to the child is severed. The children are the relative caregiver's, just as if they had been born to him or her. The child will be issued a new birth certificate with the adoptive parent's name and the adopting relative may choose to change the child's surname to match his or her own.

The adoptive parent has full discretion after the adoption is legalized to not only limit but also discontinue the child's contact with the parents. In traditional adoptions, the child is adopted into a nonrelative "stranger's" home and the parents are denied all access to their child (at least until the child turns 18, at which point the adult child may initiate a search for the parents). More recently, however, "open adoptions" are being pursued. Open adoptions allow a parent to have continuing (although often limited) contact with a child. This continued contact may involve regular face-to-face visits or may be limited to the exchange of annual letters and photographs. The biological parents and the adoptive parents sign an agreement or informal contract before the adoption is legalized, outlining what parental contact will be permitted. Unfortunately, few state legislatures and courts have yet developed a means for legally enforcing these open adoption contracts and biological parents must rely on the good faith of their child's new adoptive family.

Open adoptions may be especially appropriate in kinship care situations. Absent extreme circumstances, a kinship adoptive parent is unlikely to completely sever contact by the child's parent (the adoptive parent's offspring) with the child. Similarly, many relative caregivers are adamant about explaining to the children in their care that, "I am Grandma" and "Marie is Mom." Children raised from infancy by a relative may quite naturally address their caregiver as "Mom," but many relative caregivers are hesitant to entirely usurp this title. For this reason, adoption traditionally has been unpopular with kinship caregivers. Few family members feel the need to be legally anointed as the child's parent when they already have a familial relationship as the child's grandparent, aunt, or uncle. Similarly, terminating their adult child's parental rights signals that they have given up on that person's ability to ever stabilize his or her life or care for the children. A grandmother who adopts her grandchild must acknowledge that the sacrifice she is making is a long-term one that will continue until the child grows to adulthood.

Thus, although adoption provides the greatest level of physical and psychological stability to the child, it may also raise issues of conflicting loyalties and confusing familial relationships that deter kinship caregivers from pursuing this option. On a more practical level, adoption may be prohibitively expensive for those caregivers who have no means of paying for the court's and attorney's legal fees. Similarly, if the child is not in the child welfare system and eligible for adoption assistance funds, then the relative caregiver may experience a decrease in income following the adoption. While a grandparent's income is not counted in determining public assistance eligibility in foster care, the income is counted once the grandparent becomes the child's legal parent.

# Chapter Seven
# Federal and State
# Policy and Program Issues

The use of kinship care has rapidly grown beyond the expectations of federal and state program and policy planners. This growth has not been without problems to the child placement practices of the states.

The number of children removed from parental control and custody grew to unprecedented levels during the 1980s and early 1990s [Child Welfare League of America 1994]. State and local service systems, unable to meet demand through traditional foster and residential care programs, began to use relatives as alternative care providers in ever increasing numbers. State and federal reports of children in need of placement acknowledged that parental substance abuse and continued economic stresses increased the need for protective removals of children. States with the largest concentrations of unemployed parents and high poverty levels were hit hardest by the increased child protection demand [Children's Defense Fund 1992].

For the purposes of this chapter, *kinship care* is used to describe the specific practice of placing children with relatives by an authorized child-placing agency of state or local government. It has grown in size and form even as social service agencies struggle with costs and the adequacy of their child welfare systems.

There appears to be no consistent public policy rationale for the use and valuation of kinship care. Some conservative social policy advocates argue that government has neither a right nor a responsibility to intervene in family life, asserting that such placements are essentially family business—private arrangements that are options for caring families [Downs et al. 1996]. They suggest that relative placement arrangements are independent actions of families that should be neither directed nor controlled by government policy and regulation. These arguments also reject, in principle, the use of government funding, especially at reasonable subsistence levels, for relatives who participate in kinship placement arrangements. Their arguments typically imply that a "good relative" will care for the child without financial payment, compensation, or reimbursement, out of love for the child and a belief in strong family values.

One of the stronger arguments for expanded use of kinship homes as a placement resource is based on the value of such placements to the child. This argument does not focus on cost factors, or on the motives of families who receive funding for care, but looks solely at the child's best interests. When viewed in this light, the value of kinship care (whether treated as a family choice or as a formal component of the child welfare system) is easily determined. Kinship placements enable children to live with persons they know and trust, rather than subjecting them to the potential trauma of living with persons initially unknown to them. By keeping children connected to their families and siblings, kinship placements usually facilitate the transmission of the child's family identity and history, ethnicity, and culture. Kinship placements not only encourage families to rely on their own members, but often keep children connected to their communities and schools as well. For the individual child, one of the more important values may be that kinship placements reduce the perceived stigma attached to being labeled a "foster child," and the uncertainty and lack of public support associated with being a foster child.

As the use of kinship care has grown, kinship caregivers, usually grandparents, and less frequently, uncles and aunts, have been subjected to state and local policies and practices ranging from full support and encouragement of kinship placements to planned, intentional discouragement. As noted later in this chapter, variable legal and policy choices have created a lack of clarity regarding the circumstances of children placed with relatives by the child-placing system. Although raising a child in today's society requires, at a minimum, patience, love, understanding, and financial support, unclear or variable public policies and practices make many kinship parents feel as if their circumstances are not being appropriately addressed. Some have sought out or established support groups and other organizations that give them the opportunity to affect federal and state program policies.

The success or failure of such groups in influencing policy is closely tied to both federal and state clarification and articulation of a responsive kinship placement policy. For revised policies to become effective at the service delivery level, the leadership of child advocates, legislators, and policymakers who value keeping children connected to their families—and simultaneously safe from continued abuse or neglect—is essential.

This chapter addresses some of the arguments for and against the use of relatives as a placement option of choice for children coming into contact with the nation's child protection and out-of-home care systems. Despite some precedents in federal law, the manner in which individual states implement kinship care attests more to their financial and political perspectives than to the broader interests of keeping children connected to their families. The fundamental social policy imperative to strengthen family life is often given limited consideration in tight budgetary times. In response to a "lukewarm" federal policy on whether kinship care is a placement of choice, nearly one-half of the states have relegated relative placements to a secondary status, and have not routinely provided adequate financial and social services supports to relative caregivers, consistent with the needs of the children placed [U.S. Department of Health and Human Services 1992].

According to the U.S. Department of Health and Human Services [1992], the number of children placed with relatives increased from 18% to 31% of total foster care placements from 1986 to 1990. The growth has been greatest in urban areas, where the numbers of minority children requiring care has increased to unprecedented levels. In both New York City and Los Angeles County, for example, kinship placements comprised over 40% of all formal placements.

# Kinship Caregiver Funding

In both New York City and Los Angeles County, the local service delivery system seeks to conform its kinship care funding to federal foster care program guidelines that encourage local expenditures, matched by state and federal funds. Relatives are reimbursed at the same level as nonrelative caregivers, if they are licensed or approved, and if appropriate judicial involvement and child placing procedures have been followed.

In other states and localities, however, relatives are not routinely considered as preferred caregivers, unless they are willing to apply for AFDC benefits for the child, or meet stringent home licensing standards, similar to those applied to traditional family foster homes. In those states encouraging AFDC participation, financial and/or medical assistance is also available at rates determined by the state's AFDC standards. Kinship caregivers who receive AFDC grants receive much lower payments than licensed or certified foster parents, since AFDC benefits vary widely among states. On average, these payments are about 50% lower than foster care maintenance payments. Perhaps one of the worst examples of inequity in payments was found in Texas in 1992. This state allowed a maximum AFDC payment for one child of $75 per month, if placed with a relative. If that same child were placed in traditional foster care, the state would pay up to $554 each month to the caregiver [U.S. House of Representative Committee on Ways and Means 1993].

The practice of referring relatives to the AFDC program, if funding is desired or needed by the relative, represents a significant dollar savings to the states. It saves money by lowering foster care maintenance costs, and reducing administrative requirements. Families receiving AFDC grants, however, do not routinely receive child welfare supervision and social services assistance. AFDC benefits in this scenario are deemed by the state to be sufficient to meet the kinship caregiver's and child's needs. This approach gives little consideration to the needs of the child, particularly those children born with developmental and health-related problems. As an added administrative incentive for some states to use the AFDC grant program for children placed with relatives, kinship children are not considered a part of the state or local foster care system, and are therefore not entitled to the protections and supports required by law of state child welfare service systems. These protections might include regular supervisory and monitoring visits from the agency, case management assistance, periodic administrative case reviews, and parental involvement in case planning.

## Children in Kinship Families

Accurate information about children in kinship family situations is difficult to obtain, given the number of informal or voluntary family arrangements, and the underreporting of formal placements by state and local government agencies. According to the U.S. Bureau of the Census [1993], the number of children under the age of 18 living with grandparents grew from a reported 2.2 million in 1972 to approximately 3.3 million in 1992. A total of 4.3 million children were reported as living with all types of relatives in 1992. Most population projections suggest continued increases in the number of children placed with relatives, if social and economic factors such as out-of-wedlock births, separations, divorces, family violence, and unemployment continue to increase in a community.

U.S. Bureaus of the Census data [1993] on the racial composition of children in kinship families indicate that African American children are more likely than others to live in the home of a grandparent. In 1992, nearly 5% of all children lived in grandparent-headed households. Approximately 12% of African American children lived in grandparent-headed homes, while less than 4% of Caucasian children lived in such homes.

Some observers and critics of current public social policy development suggest that if kinship placements were a dominant practice among Caucasian majority families, clear and concise federal and state policy guidance would have been articulated and implemented long ago. Those who plan and implement services to children should address this dilemma at both state and local service delivery levels, as welfare policy is assessed, since the vast majority of children reported for suspected abuse and neglect (and who enter the child welfare system) are already known to the welfare system.

Limited research has been commissioned in the area of kinship care, when compared with the volumes of literature compiled about traditional foster care. Some research findings suggest that children placed with relatives remain in care for longer periods of time than children in traditional foster care. Several explanations have been offered for this disparity: (1) parents of children in kinship placements have reduced access to services, (2) quality family reunification services are not being made available to this population, (3) relatives desire to keep the children out of foster care, and (4) diligent permanency planning efforts for this group of children are lacking.

## Kinship Care in New York City

A 1991 unpublished survey of 11,600 children in formal kinship care placements, conducted by New York City's Child Welfare Administration, found that the average length of stay was longer by at least one year for children in kinship care than for those placed in traditional foster care. Case record reviews conducted by the child-serving agencies noted that permanency planning goals identified for these kinship placements were: return to biological parent (75%), adoption (18%), and discharge to a relative, independent living, or adult residential living (7%). For the majority of children in kinship care, the child-serving agency established a return to family goal. In many instances, however, the records did not reflect that sound services were available or provided to the parent to facilitate the achievement of this goal.

The ages of the children in kinship care in New York City were also significant, in terms of determining resource, service, and support needs. Of the children in the survey, 30% were under three years of age, 24% were ages three to six, 18% were between the ages of seven and nine , and 17% were age 10 to 13. Only 11% of the children in kinship care were age 14 or older. The age issue was felt to be significant in view of the health care, child care, and educational needs of the younger children, and the associated costs incurred by their kinship parents.

The New York City survey also reviewed the primary reasons for the child's placement. In most cases, multiple factors resulted in a petition to remove the child from parental custody. By far the largest single factor influencing placement decisions was parental substance abuse, present in 77% of the kinship cases. Findings of general neglect (14%), mental illness (3%), physical abuse (2%), and abandonment (2%) were also documented as the primary causes for removal and placement. The remaining 3% of the children entered kinship care as a result of sexual abuse, emotional neglect, or the death, hospitalization, or incarceration of their parent.

The records clearly indicated direct relationships between children entering the kinship care system (and traditional care systems as well) to other service systems. It is impossible to separate foster care from policy decisions (and policy consequences for children) in the areas of welfare, mental health, health, juvenile justice, law enforcement, judicial, and legal practices. Given the common denominator of poverty, many of the above-mentioned programs and service practices were not targeted to kinship placements, and may have contributed to the length of time required to effect family reunification. It should be expected that when kinship placements are used, many of the families will require assistance and services if return to parents is a part of the service plan. Their problems and needs are consistent with those of many of the most needy families in the community, who are already known to existing service systems.

## Limitations of Traditional Foster Care

In nearly every state, the supply of licensed family foster homes has not kept pace with the demand for placement. Some states report that these limits are resulting in a reconsideration of relative home utilization. Others note that the needs of many children entering care appear to be increasingly complex, and that many foster parents are not adequately trained and supported in coping with the problems observed in seriously abused and neglected children. They cite the children's extensive emotional, medical, behavioral, and developmental needs as among the problems that are causing foster parents to question their effectiveness and continued involvement as care providers.

Retention and development of foster parents has been an issue of concern over many years. A 1989 report by the U.S. General Accounting Office identified factors contributing to high foster parent turnover rates, including the poor public image of foster care, low state reimbursement levels for foster parents, increased labor force participation of women who might have previously provided full-time foster care, and inadequate support services to foster parents. The GAO report suggested that these issues may also impact foster parent retention as well as recruitment rates. According to a report made to the National Foster Parents Association at their annual conference in 1994, nearly 30% of licensed foster parents leave caregiving annually. Recruitment and retention problems in traditional foster care have not been a critical problem in those states developing comprehensive kinship care policies and practices.

## Federal Policy Influences

### *The Adoption Assistance and Child Welfare Act of 1980*

The Adoption Assistance and Child Welfare Act of 1980 (P.L. 96-272) has been cited as a support to the emergence of kinship care. This legislation was developed in response to national conditions in child welfare during the 1970s. A review of the U.S. House of Representatives Committee on Ways and Means Report on H.R. 3434 details a number of problems found in traditional foster care services. Lawmakers expressed concern that too many children were languishing in foster care for too long, some becoming lost in the system; too many children were being removed from their homes and placed in inappropriate and unnecessary foster and residential care placements; and services to the parents of children in care were often nonexistent. Placement prevention services to parents were not routinely available. Adoption opportunities, particularly for special needs and older children, were limited. Children were believed to be languishing in care for lack of adequate case planning, regular case review, services to prevent removal from their parents, and reunification activity.

While foster care was considered a necessary service for many children, the 1980 reforms required states to provide preventive services to avert removals, and to seek the least restrictive, most family-like setting available when removal could not be averted. Additional matching federal funds were made available to states to provide adoption subsidies for hard-to-place and special-needs children where return to the parent was not a viable option.

When the child welfare reform bill originally passed the House of Representatives, there was a requirement that states give preference to relatives as foster care providers. The Committee Report accompanying the bill noted that federally reimbursed foster care would be available to relatives under certain conditions. The final bill did not include specific references to the relative preference issue, however. Many states interpreted Congressional intent and the reforms as intent to include relatives, and enacted state policies that gave relatives some preferences, under the "most family-like setting" and "least restrictive placement" requirements contained in the law. In nearly one-half of the states, relatives were given consideration as a placement resource. Relative or kinship homes were considered to be "less-restrictive" than traditional family foster care placements.

## *Title IV-B and Title IV-E*

Federal child welfare policy is also set forth in Title IV-B and Title IV-E of the Social Security Act and subsequent amendments. Title IV-B authorizes federal matching funds of 75% for the provision of certain foster care services and for the protection for children in care. In 1993, a new subpart 2 was added to Title IV-B that provided funds to states to plan and develop family preservation and support services. Extended families were explicitly included as eligible for services under these new provisions. Services for families at risk of losing their children to foster care, and community-based family support services, were included in the types of programs supportable by federal funds, if the states chose to include them in their operating plans.

These initiatives, contained in the Family Preservation and Family Support Act of 1993, were intended as a "capped entitlement." Under the provisions of the act, each state is entitled to a share of appropriated dollars, subject to a national spending ceiling established by Congress. The formula that determines a state's funding share to provide these services is considered by some to be inequitable, since it is calculated based upon the number of federal Food Stamp recipients in the state as of a specific date.

Title IV-E of the Social Security Act authorizes states to receive matching funds on an "open-ended entitlement" basis without predetermined limits. The costs of maintaining children in foster care whose parents are eligible for AFDC are included in these provisions. Nearly one-half of all children in foster care are believed to be AFDC eligible. The reimbursement rates to states for foster care maintenance are identical to each state's AFDC and Medicaid rate. Title IV-E, like most of Title IV-B, does not explicitly include kinship care as a reimbursable cost to the state. It is a state option, however, that progressive policy and program planners are selecting as one means of developing more effective kinship and family strengthening programs.

The Family Preservation and Family Support Act has the potential to provide supportive services that may facilitate placement of children with family members. Placement with relatives with federal support, as an alternative to traditional care, is one way of strengthening families. Specifically, Section 425(a)(1), of the Social Security Act contains provisions that support services designed to "prevent the unnecessary separation of children from their families by identifying family problems, assisting them in resolving them, and preventing breakup of families where the prevention of removal is desirable and possible."

## Aid to Families with Dependent Children (AFDC)

The placement of a child with relatives, whether voluntarily or involuntarily, is a traumatic circumstance for the child, parents, and relatives. Often such placements have serious economic implications for the caregiving family. Many would also argue that involvement in the public assistance system for what is basically a "child assistance allowance" is problematic, given public opinion and attitudes about the welfare system and those who receive it.

In the past, some states have used Title IV-A of the Social Security Act and the AFDC financial grant system to cover the costs of kinship care. Rather than designing a system consistent with child welfare services and objectives for children placed with relatives, these states chose to funnel interested relatives into their public assistance programs. There are extreme variations among state AFDC payment levels, just as there are among state foster care maintenance levels. Relatives who were funneled into the AFDC system for financial assistance were normally reimbursed at a much lower rate than if they had been offered comprehensive kinship foster care services.

Subsequent to the passage of major welfare reforms and the elimination of the entitlement aspects of the AFDC programs, states have submitted proposed operating plans to the U.S. Department of Health and Human Services for the use of TANF (Targeted Assistance to Needy Families) grants. The manner in which kinship care providers, previously referred to AFDC, will be handled is now a state-level determination. Whether states will develop alternative funding sources for this special group of relatives or exempt persons in this group from work requirements contained in the new legislation must be reviewed on a state-by-state basis.

## Waivers

During 1995, a notice published by the U.S. Department of Health and Human Services announced the availability of federal waivers of certain sections of the Social Security Act to allow states to experiment with alternative approaches to the provision of child welfare services, including more creative use of kinship care. This action may signal acknowledgment of the growing importance of providing more effective services to families, and to the importance of building a continuum of services in state child welfare systems.

To date, accurate national and regional information about kinship care and its various forms, and clarity about what constitutes acceptable policy and practice, has not been accumulated. A substantial investment in research is necessary to obtain accurate, timely, and appropriate information about service needs and outcomes. The absence of quantifiable data is allowing anecdotal and "worst case" reports to guide and inform policy. During periods of heightened debate about the values and benefits of social program spending, such information deficits give aid and comfort to those who would demean and dismantle programs serving the poor for economic purposes. The consequences for children in need of assistance are too often overlooked in the debates to reduce government expenditures for the poor.

Through the use of waivers of certain federal requirements in order to experiment with varying service models, agency practice and program flexibility can be improved. A targeted investment in research (both agency and university based) could lead to the establishment of a knowledge base that would inform policy at the federal, regional, and state levels. This knowledge could lead to the development of training materials for the preparation of workers serving kinship family systems.

## State Policy Directions

Given resource shortages and pressures to reduce taxes, many state governments are reviewing their social service program expenditures and related federal mandates. In 1996, Congress passed and the President signed into law a reform of welfare entitlements. The legislation essentially eliminated the AFDC system, and established new state options, such as the length of time a family may receive Temporary Assistance to Needy Families (TANF) funding, but did not address the issue of states that have previously used AFDC to assist relatives raising children.

Revising current financial reimbursement schemes and matching formulas, and the consolidation of separate federal programs into block grants to states will enable each state to determine its priorities and how best to address them programmatically. State-level policymakers and program advocates will have greater opportunity to reassess allocation and reallocation priorities.

As significant federal reforms are enacted by the Congress, however, one can assume that the total federal dollars available to states for child and family services will be less than current levels over time. There is a strong likelihood that kinship care, its value to children, and the importance of this system of care to minority families will be targeted for reductions, if historical patterns are maintained. This possibility suggests that advocates must learn to package and present state and local family needs information more effectively. If kinship services are to remain a relevant component of the state child welfare system, state policy developers must look beyond gross financial concerns and put a renewed emphasis on strengthening family ties and connections.

Many of the arguments supporting state block grant funding strategies included such issues as allowing greater overall flexibility, less federal intrusion into state operations, less bureaucracy, and fewer program mandates. While some of these arguments may well be specious, one should note that in the broader welfare reform debates of 1995, there was scarce notice or discussion of kinship care, and the unprecedented growth of this form of placement. It is unclear whether states will be encouraged to design and develop responsive kinship policies, programs, and services. There are, however, some important questions and issues to be raised in every state, by advocates for abused and neglected children, by parent advocates, and by policymakers.

Before a clear and coherent state policy can be developed, and responsive programs designed, there must be agreement on terminology. Not only is there confusion in what to call kinship care, there is a lack of common acceptance of the essential components of a kinship care system. A review of various state policies reveals that such terms as *relative family care, home of relative placements, extended family care, relative foster care,* and *kinship foster care* are used to describe both payment options and placement practices. These differing terms also reflect differing philosophies underlying service design and delivery. It should be remembered that traditional foster care systems were designed with strangers in mind. The use of unrelated caregivers was the design intent, and may well continue to be the dominant influence whenever kinship care policy is discussed, unless state planners become more focused on the value of kinship to children, rather than solely on economic and administrative efficiencies.

Given the issues discussed above, state child protective and placement systems will have few choices other than to develop kinship care
programs, if current trends continue. The placement of children with
relatives, while less restrictive than traditional family foster care placements, could be enhanced by many of the protections and supports
available to children in traditional family foster care. This is not to suggest
that kinship care and foster care are identical, or that the systems should
necessarily be combined into a single service structure. Rather, states
should view kinship care systems in the context of a continuum of care for
abused, neglected, and at-risk children.

States must be willing to review current practices, and to define and
refine relative recruitment and screening techniques now in place. Resolving the question of whether relative homes should meet identical or a
modified version of standards and requirements for unrelated foster
homes is a critical first step. While methods and means to determine
physical and environmental safety, moral fitness and character, and the
caregiver's ability to protect and nurture the child must be addressed in
state kinship care policy, recognition must also be given to the reality that
there is a practice difference between the treatment of relatives and the
treatment of strangers in most out-of-home care systems.

Activities such as thorough home studies, orientation and training of
kinship providers, and relationships with the supervising agency must be
detailed in state program guidelines. As a general rule, state agencies must
recognize that relative caregivers, for the most part, have prior relationships with the child and biological parents. They will most likely maintain
contact and involvement with both parties long after formal agency
involvement is discontinued. In addressing child protection and safety of
children from continuing parental abuse, service strategies and staff
development must be developed to enlist proactive relative assistance,
which anticipates and defuses potential problem situations. Foster parents
have long been viewed as active partners with service agencies; the same
principle should be applied to kinship caregivers.

In designing formal kinship care structures, states will need to
confront a range of negative assumptions about the appropriateness of
relatives as care providers. Administrators, supervisors, and direct care

workers should be encouraged to openly discuss their observations and beliefs about the "dysfunctional family" and how these notions may influence program offerings and placement preferences. In some states, "bad seed" theorists continue to dominate and influence such discussions. To balance such debate, state planning efforts should include active engagement of experienced kinship providers and advocates, and such national organizations as the American Association of Retired Persons, the National Conference on the Aging, the Child Welfare League of America, and Generations United, as well as local organizations.

Supporters of strong kinship care policy at the state level express concern that many states tend to design policies that serve the best interests of the bureaucracy, rather than those of children and families. When addressing kinship issues, states must naturally consider multicultural service provisions issues. Added care must be taken, however, to separate the requirement to consider families as a preferred resource for many children from the current ideological debate surrounding affirmative action and perceived preferential treatment, and benefits to minority populations. While controversial, kinship care—and the service policies that strengthen it—should become the first option considered when child placement is necessary, regardless of racial or cultural characteristics. Public education, staff training, kinship parent training, and orientation programs must be developed to facilitate program improvement at the state and local levels of service delivery.

State program activities should also include establishing collaborative relationships with the range of educational and service organizations serving children and families in kinship care. Given the needs of the children entering care for protective purposes, and the problems many of their families encounter, interdisciplinary approaches to service provision must be established and implemented at all levels.

## Permanency Planning in Kinship Care

Since the implementation of the federal Adoption Assistance and Child Welfare Act of 1980 (P.L. 96-272), child welfare agencies have sought to establish and implement goals that will result in children being placed in stable permanent home settings. In all states, the goal of "return to parent" is the most frequently identified and achieved outcome. Adoption has also been established as a legitimate outcome for children whose parental rights have been terminated.

In regard to children placed with relatives, the adoption goal has caused confusion, and anxiety for relatives, children, and agency personnel. In many instances, delays in adoptive placement occur due to the time required to legally terminate parental rights. In a number of states, kinship parents as possible adoptive parents are not given high priority. In others, children placed with relatives are informally considered to be in long-term placement, and termination proceedings are not initiated routinely. Long-term relative placement as a legitimate permanency planning goal should be considered in jurisdictions with large kinship care populations.

In some states concerned with the increasing number of children in long-term kinship placements, efforts to encourage kinship adoptions have been undertaken. Underlying these concerns is a belief that children are better off in adoptive situations, where legal protections are available to both the child and the adoptive parent. This approach assumes that adoption is as desirable an outcome for kinship children and their families as it is for a child with no available family ties. It also assumes that adoption is in the best interests of the agency. These efforts, while laudable, miss the essence of kinship care, and confuse the needs of children in traditional foster care with those who are placed with relatives. Kinship children are not without permanent family. Many kinship family members resist and reject the procedural aspects of adoption, particularly activities leading to the termination of parental rights. Others are unable to afford the costs of attorneys and adoption home studies without government assistance.

With strong encouragement from agencies, and the use of subsidies and postadoption services, many grandparents are agreeing to adopt children who have lived in their homes for extended periods of time. They are often reluctant participants in a process that is frequently more important to the child welfare agency than to the family's vision of successful outcomes for their child. Relative adoptions can be successful, however, when all parties focus on the child's interests, and a supportive system of services and supports to adoptive parents is in place and operational.

## Action Steps for State and Local Planners

A state-level planning group or commission should be convened to conduct a thorough review of state policy and practices regarding kinship care and to devise a strategic plan and action system. This group should be broad-based, culturally sensitive, informed, and committed to ensuring adequate treatment of all children placed with relatives. Judges, attorneys, direct service agency representatives, educators, and others who serve children and families should be involved in this planning process. The impact of kinship care on special interests, such as traditional care and residential care lobbies, should also be understood. Traditional care providers should be carefully involved in the planning process.

State universities should be encouraged to conduct demographic research with families involved in both informal and formal kinship care. Additional information, factual presentations, and objective analysis of the service needs of children entering care through child protective proceedings must be developed to better inform taxpayers and the policymakers of unmet needs, and how kinship services may be used to meet those needs.

Financial support policies should be assessed to ensure that they are adequate and sufficient to meet the basic needs of children in care. Quality kinship care should not be considered a cost containment or cost-neutral service activity. Financial policies should emphasize that any support offered to a kinship parent is not a salary for services rendered, but a reimbursement for a portion of the costs involved in caring for the child. The cost to states will be much higher if more restrictive child placement settings are used.

An analysis of funding sources in use and those available to the state should be undertaken. Consideration must be given to efforts to maximize federal funding opportunities, such as those contained in the Family

Preservation and Support Act initiatives and in federally funded foster care opportunities that stress services to keep children with their families.

The receipt of public funds for the care of children confers special obligations on state governments, state child welfare agencies, funding recipients, and extended family members. Participation in agency training, supervision, and information exchanges designed to ensure adequate child protection and safety, and to promote normal child growth and development, is a responsibility of every caregiver, and should be explicitly contained in a formal contract executed between the caregiver and supervising agency. Supervising agencies must commit sufficient resources to monitoring care providers and child progress.

All staff who work directly with kinship children and their families should receive comprehensive, culturally sensitive, competency-based specialized training. Family systems and the use of group processes in serving families should be components of the training curriculum. Such training should be developed and/or approved by the state agency and provided uniformly on a statewide basis.

Community-based and preventive services should be made known and available to kinship families in areas where voluntary or informal placements are made outside of the jurisdiction of a state's child protective services and foster care system. The availability of such services may reduce the escalation of problems and the need for subsequent state agency or judicial intervention.

## Summary

The potential of kinship care systems and networks has yet to be fully realized and fully integrated into the formal child welfare placement system. As legal and regulatory requirements are clarified, state and local delivery systems will need to be revised and new approaches developed. While there are many similarities in the service needs of children in kinship care and those in traditional family foster care, there are also major differences. Service strategies that maximize the familiarity of the kinship family with the child's situation are being developed in many states.

Kinship placements should be considered as an integral part of a continuum of placement options available for the protection of vulnerable children. Every jurisdiction needs to assess its recruitment, retention, and support system for providers. Ongoing training, assistance in functioning as a part of an agency team, and an adequate reimbursement system are essential elements of a responsive kinship care system.

Kinship care is an emotionally charged service program, given current values and attitudes about the poor, their capacity, and their potential. The absence of solid data about kinship care only adds to the confusion. Clearly, outcome data for the entire child welfare system is not encouraging, and rigorous investigation is needed. Supporters of kinship care, as well as its detractors, agree that children need more services and targeted assistance than they are currently receiving. How we as a nation and society address this dilemma may well determine the lifetime opportunities for thousands of our nation's most vulnerable children. Providing responsive services for children placed with relatives is one measure of our nation's compassion and commitment to our future.

When the final record of the late 1990s social welfare policy is written, a portion of that record, it is hoped, will detail more creative efforts by both federal and state governments to assist families in caring for dependent relatives. Kinship care, a unique development of an overwhelmed and crisis-driven child welfare system, may yet become a force for stabilizing children who might otherwise be set adrift.

# Appendix
# *A Kinship Care Case Study*[*]

The case study highlighted in this appendix provides an example of the clinical issues impacting kinship families and the implementation of intervention strategies and goals. Household members in this case study include 11-year-old Mark, Mrs. G (Mark's 68-year-old paternal grandmother), Mr. G (Mark's 32-year-old father), Aunt G (Mark's 34-year-old paternal aunt), and Gerald (Aunt G's son and Mark's cousin).

## Background

Mark was placed with his paternal grandmother, Mrs. G, two years ago, after having been physically abused by his mother. Mark's mother assaulted him with a hammer after he refused to give her the money he had earned from delivering newspapers to support her crack addiction. Mark's mother and father were separated at the time of the incident.

Mrs. G is now 68 years old and suffers from high blood pressure. She accepted temporary guardianship for Mark under the assumption that her son, Mr. G, would regain custody of Mark. The local Department of Human Services (DHS) now has custody of Mark, since Mark's mother was incarcerated for child abuse and Mr. G could not be found at the time of the incident. Mr. G recently returned temporarily to his mother's home.

---

[*] This case vignette is extracted with permission from the "Kids 'N' Kin" kinship program of the Philadelphia Society for Services to Children. Identifying information has been changed to protect the privacy of the clients.

Mr. G is currently unemployed and has a drinking problem. His stated goals to DHS are to: (1) find employment, (2) get into substance abuse treatment, (3) obtain housing, and (4) regain custody of Mark.

Also living in the household are Aunt G and her son Gerald. Aunt G has been living with her mother, Mrs. G for the past six years. She contributes to the household by (1) paying her mother rent, (2) sharing household expenses (i.e., electricity, phone, gas, food), (3) acting as a secondary caregiver for Mark, and (4) helping her mother with her medical needs. Aunt G resents her brother "using" their mother and feels he should be responsible for housing and caring for Mark and himself. She insists on not letting her brother also use her. Aunt G feels that taking care of Mark is enough and that taking him in is acceptable since he is an "innocent child."

Mrs. G is hopeful that her son will "get himself together." She is trying to be helpful and patient until he can find independent living arrangements for himself and Mark. She is ambivalent about assuming full custody because of her faith in her son, her medical problems, and her limited income from Social Security.

Significant others in Mark's life include Mark's maternal grandmother and his mother, whom he visits once a month when she stays at his maternal grandmother's home on weekend furloughs. Mark is hoping to live with his mother or father. Mark does periodically defy Mrs. G's and his aunt's authority. Mark's mother will not be released from prison for three more years. Mark feels responsible and guilty for her incarceration. He refuses to be alone with her because of his fear of her physical retaliation.

## Individual Interventions

The worker for the G family is under court order to establish permanent custody and residency for Mark in four months. To do so successfully, the worker will need to intervene with individual family members, including Mark's paternal grandmother, aunt, father, and mother, as well as with Mark himself.

*Interventions with the paternal grandmother (Mrs. G) should be planned to help her:*

- interrupt her codependent relationship (as an enabler) with her son (Mr. G—an active alcoholic);

- enhance her skills in interrupting the family's legacy of (1) alcohol abuse by male family members, and (2) females enabling alcohol abuse, which Mrs. G began in her relationship with her husband (Mark's paternal grandfather, now deceased);

- minimize her split loyalties so that she begins identifying her grandson's needs as a priority over those of her son;

- develop goals for her son and a timetable in which to accomplish them, in order for him to remain in her home or regain custody of his son;

- resolve her fantasies of her son "getting himself together," so that she will pursue custody of her grandson;

- cope with her guilt (as an enabler) for her son's substance abuse, so that she will not allow him to live in her home as long as he is drug dependent;

- accept the possibility that her son might do worse if he left her home, and that he will have no motivation to change if he remains in her home; and

- accept Mark's need to be involved with his mother and maternal extended family, therefore minimizing sabotage and competition with Mark's mother and maternal grandmother.

*Interventions with Mark's father (Mr. G) should be planned to help him:*

- place his son's needs before his own (using a child-focused approach as motivation);

- obtain a room in a boarding home and focus on getting treatment (using an individual approach as motivation);

- minimize his sabotage of or competition with his mother for custody (using a child and individual approach); and

- give Mark permission to accept his grandmother and aunt's authority.

*Interventions with Mark's mother should be planned to help her (with the help of her counselor in prison):*

- accept responsibility for abusing her son (Mark);

- accept Mark's right to refuse to give her money for her addiction;

- accept Mark's right to be angry and fearful of her;

- acknowledge the need to exonerate Mark of any guilt or responsibility for her incarceration;

- resolve her fantasy of Mark's immediate return to her following her release from prison; and

- relinquish custody of Mark to his paternal grandmother (using an individual and child focus approach), therefore minimizing competition or sabotage.

*Interventions with Mark's Aunt G should be planned to help her:*

- resolve past issues with her mother (Mrs. G) related to her enabling her father (and now her brother) to abuse drugs and alcohol at the expense of her children;

- not accept an enabling role with her brother; and

- not accept being a secondary caregiver or being the alternative caregiver if Mrs. G allowed her brother to remain in the home drug or alcohol dependent.

*Interventions with Mark should be planned to help him:*

- minimize his feelings of guilt about his mother's incarceration and his not wanting to return to her;

- validate his right to feel angry with and fearful of his mother;

- discontinue his role as an enabler by helping him to admit and not excuse his mother and father's drug and alcohol addiction;

- acknowledge and validate his feelings of not wanting to live with his father while drug or alcohol dependent, therefore minimizing his fantasy of returning to live with his mother or father; and

- engage in a loss and grief process about his absent parents.

## Dyad Interventions

The worker should engage in dyad interventions with (1) Mrs. G and her daughter Aunt G; (2) Mrs. G and her son Mr. G; (3) Mark and his father; (4) Mark and his mother; and (5) Mrs. G and Mark's maternal grandmother. Triad interventions will result if other professionals become involved.

*Interventions with Mrs. G and her daughter should have as their goal:*

- Mrs. G's acknowledgment and acceptance of her daughter's anger about being expendable during childhood due to Mrs. G's enabling and her father's alcohol abuse;

- Mrs. G's commitment to her daughter to protect her grandchildren (Mark and Gerald) from being expendable or exposed to her son's (Mark's father) drug and alcohol dependency (the family legacy); and

- the development of an alternative permanency plan in anticipation of Mrs. G's illness or death (mortality, morbidity, and respite plans).

*Interventions with Mrs. G and her son should have as their goal:*

- the development of a contract, timetable, and conditions for Mr. G remaining in Mrs. G's home or regaining custody of Mark (using a child and individual focus approach); and

- Mrs. G confronting her son about not meeting his contract, toward the end of Mrs. G acquiring custody of her grandson Mark and not allowing Mr. G to reside in her home while he remains drug dependent.

*Interventions with Mark and his father should have as their goal:*

- engaging Mark and his father in a loss and grief process that will redefine their contact and communication and Mr. G's involvement with Mark (i.e., visits);

- Mr. G reinforcing Mrs. G's and Aunt G's authority by having Mr. G direct Mark to "respect his grandmother and aunt" (minimizing Mark's sabotaging, testing, or feelings of disloyalty);

- Mr. G minimizing Mark's fantasies by explaining to Mark that he would be "better off with his grandmother because his boarding room wasn't large enough for both of them and that they wouldn't live together right away"; and

- Mr. G's minimizing Mark's projections and anger with his grandmother by explaining that Mr. G's leaving "Grandmom's" was his decision because he needed to "get some things together."

*Interventions with Mark and his mother during her weekend furloughs from prison should have as their goal:*

- Mark's mother acknowledging to him that her abuse of him was wrong;

- Mark's mother validating to Mark his right to not give her his money for her drug problem (thereby exonerating Mark of guilt);

- Mark's mother validating to Mark his right to be fearful of her or not wanting to live with her following her release;

- Mark's mother informing Mark of a "halfway" program at which she'd be living following her release (thereby minimizing his fantasies and fears of living with her);

- Mark's mother exonerating Mark of any responsibility for her incarceration;

- Mark's mother allowing Mark to not see her alone during her furloughs because of his fear of her retaliation; and

- Mark's mother identifying a process for reestablishing Mark's trust in her.

*Interventions with Mrs. G and Mark's maternal grandmother should have as their goal:*

- the acknowledgment of Mark's need to be involved with his mother, father, and their extended families (using a child focus approach);

- clarifying for each other and for Mark the hierarchy for decision making and authority;

- establishing lines of communication between the two families;

- determining how Mark will be involved in and communicate with his maternal extended family (i.e., phone calls, visits, holidays); and

- providing Mark with a safe and protected environment when visiting his mother during her furloughs.

# *Bibliography*

Ackerman, N. J. (1980). The family with adolescents. In E. A. Carter & M. McGoldrick (Eds.), *The family life cycle: A framework for family therapy*. New York: Gardner Press.

Administration for Children, Youth and Families. (1991). *Information memorandum on relative foster care*. Washington, DC: U.S. Department of Health and Human Services (#ACYF IM-91-11, Mat).

American Public Welfare Association. (1990). *Characteristics of children in substitute and adoptive care: A statistical summary of the VCIS National Child Welfare Data Base*. Washington, DC: Author.

Beckerman, A. (1994). Mothers in prison: Meeting the prerequisite conditions for permanency planning. *Social Work, 39,* 9–14.

Center for the Study of Social Policy. (1990). *Keeping troubled families together: Promising programs and statewide reform*. Washington, DC: The Family Impact Seminar.

Center for the Study of Social Policy. (1990). *The crisis in foster care*. Washington, DC: The Family Impact Seminar.

Child Welfare League of America. (1988). *Standards for health care services for children in out-of-home care*. Washington, DC: Author.

Child Welfare League of America. (1994). *Kinship care: A natural bridge*. Washington, DC: Author.

Crumbley, J. (1985). Child and adolescent maltreatment: Implications for family therapy. In M. Mirkin & S. Koman (Eds.), *Handbook of adolescent and family therapy.* New York: Gardner Press.

Dubowitz, H., Feigelman, S., Zuravin, S., Tepper, V., Davidson, N., & Lichenstein, R. (in press). The physical health of children in kinship care. *American Journal of Diseases of Children.*

Dubowitz, H., Tepper, V., Feigelman, S., Sawyer, R., & Davidson, N. (1990). *The physical and mental health and education status of children placed with relatives— Final report.* Prepared for the Maryland Department of Human Resources and the Baltimore City Department of Social Services. Baltimore, MD: Author.

Guerin, P. J. (1976). *Family therapy: Theory and practice.* New York: Gardner Press.

Hafner, G. (1991, July/August). Protections extended to foster children in kinship care. *Youth Law News.*

Haley, J. (1973). *Uncommon therapy: The psychiatric techniques of Milton H. Erickson, M.D.* New York: Norton.

Hoffman, L. (1981). *Foundations of family therapy.* New York: Basic Books.

Kaufman, E., & Kaufman, P. (1979). *Family therapy of drug and alcohol abuse.* New York: Gardner Press.

Madanes, C. (1981). *Strategic family therapy.* San Francisco: Jossey-Bass.

Meyers, B. S., & Link, M. K. (1990). *Kinship foster care: The double-edged dilemma.* Rochester, NY: Task Force on Permanency Planning for Foster Children, Inc.

Mirviss, M., & Hafner, G. (1992). *Baltimore's kinship foster care litigation: Why this way?"* Baltimore: Legal Aid Bureau.

Napier, A. Y., & Whitaker, C. A. (1978). *The family crucible.* New York: Harper & Row.

National Black Child Development Institute, Inc. (1989). *Who will care when parents can't? A study of Black children in foster care.* Washington, DC: Author.

National Commission on Family Foster Care. (1991). *A blueprint for fostering infants, children and youth in the 1990s.* Washington, DC: Child Welfare League of America.

National Commission on Family Foster Care. (1991). *A blueprint for fostering infants, children, and youth in the 1990s.* Washington, DC: Child Welfare League of America.

Neal, L. (1992). *An African American perspective on kinship foster care.* New York: New York Chapter, Association of Black Social Workers Child Adoption Counseling and Referral Services.

New York State Child Welfare Training Institute. (1993). Issues in kinship and foster family adoptions. In *Helping children through the adoption process.* Buffalo, NY: Center for Development of Human Services, State University of Buffalo.

Nichols, M. P. (1984). *Family therapy: Concepts and methods.* New York: Gardner Press.

Philadelphia Society for Services to Children. (1993). *A handbook for relative caregivers.* Philadelphia: Author

Section 425(a)(1), Social Security Act (42 U.S.C. 625).

Stack, C. (1974). *All our kin: Strategies for survival in a Black community.* New York: Harper and Row.

Stanton, M. D., Todd, T. C., & Associates. (1982). *The family therapy of drug abuse and addiction.* New York: Guilford.

Thornton, J. L. (1987). *Investigation into the nature of the kinship foster home* (doctoral dissertation, Yeshiva University, New York, NY).

Thornton, J. L. (1991). Permanency planning for children in kinship foster homes. *Child Welfare 70,* 593–601.

U.S. Bureau of Census. (1993). *Current population reports 1992.* Washington, DC: U.S. Government Printing Office.

U.S. Department of Health and Human Services, Office of Inspector General. (1992). *Using relatives for foster care.* Washington, DC: U.S. Government Printing Office (OEI-06-90-02390).

U.S. General Accounting Office. (1989). *Foster parents: Recruiting and preservice training practices need evaluation* (pp. 13–14). Washington, DC: Author (HRD-89-86).

U.S. House of Representatives Committee on Ways and Means Committee. (1979). H.R. Report 96-136.

U.S. House of Representatives Committee on Ways and Means. (1993). *Overview of entitlement programs: 1993 greenbook* (pp. 659–669, 896–897). Washington, DC: U.S. Government Printing Office.

Visher, E. B., & Visher, J. S. (1979). *Stepfamilies: A guide to working with stepparents and stepchildren.* New York: Brunner/Mazel.

Wilson, D. B., & Chipungu, S. S. (Eds.) (1996). Kinship care. *Child Welfare, 75* (Special Issue).

Woody, J. D., & Woody, R. H. (Eds.). (1983). *Sexual issues in family therapy.* Rockville, MD: Aspen.